The **Na** Bachelor

You reference guide for London!!
Enjoy yourself.

John & Satomi xxx

September 2003

"I only ever use Darrel Bristow-Bovey's recipes."

— BRUCE FORDYCE, MULTIPLE WINNER OF
THE COMRADES ULTRA-MARATHON

"I look at Darrel Bristow-Bovey and I wonder what my life will be like when I am his age. And even if it is not a Sunday, I go down on my knees and say a little prayer." — GARETH CLIFF, 702 DRIVE-SHOW HOST

"When I first saw a copy of *The Naked Bachelor*, I sent a copy to everyone I know and I said: "You see! This is why it is important to wear clothes!"
— NADINE RUBIN, EDITOR, SOUTH AFRICAN *ELLE*

"I would not sleep with Darrel Bristow-Bovey if he was the last man on earth." — ILSE-MARIE FROM *BIG BROTHER*

"Although he pretends otherwise, Darrel is a connoisseur of food. Even before I ring the doorbell, he always knows if the guys in the kitchen have remembered his standing order of extra cheese. You can't fool him. He is like the Rain Man of takeaways."

— DON, THE DEBONAIRS DELIVERY GUY

"Follow the yellow brick road! Follow the yellow brick road!"
— GWEN GILL, SOCIAL COLUMNIST

"Darrel Bristow-Bovey is not welcome in our organisation."

— ZANU-PF

"There is a cold, no, a hot, no, a cold ... um ... yes, a cold front over Cape Town." — SIMON GEAR, WEATHERMAN

"I would like to return our order of *I Moved Your Cheese*. There seems to have been some mistake."

— ANY NUMBER OF SOUTH AFRICAN CORPORATE
PERSONNEL DIRECTORS

"I wouldn't say I am disappointed with the second book, exactly. My expectations weren't all that high. I am glad there's no cheese in this one. I never really understood about the cheese. People would ask: 'What's with your son and cheese?' and I wouldn't know what to say. There was never all that much cheese in the house, to tell you the truth. We weren't a big cheese-eating family, no matter what he tells people in those interviews. I hate to say this, but sometimes he isn't honest. Now I know what Eminem's mother must go through. At least he spelt my name correctly this time."
— ROSSLYN BRISTOW-BOVEY, THE AUTHOR'S MOTHER

"Wicked."
— JAMIE OLIVER

"Naked is as naked does."
— FORREST GUMP

"I heartily endorse this book. I haven't read it, or the first book. Or any book, actually. But I know Darrel to be a man of principle. I always say, 'Darrel, have an egg on that burger,' and he always says, 'No, I don't like eggs.' And he has never gone back on that. Never. I am from Australia."
— MIKE HAYSMAN, FORMER CRICKETER,
TELEVISION PRESENTER, AUSTRALIAN

"Why are there so few black people represented on this page?"
— LETTER WRITER, THE *STAR* NEWSPAPER

"I still think there is something wrong with Darrel Bristow-Bovey."
— TIM MODISE, MEDIA PERSONALITY, CHAIRMAN OF
PROUDLY SOUTH AFRICAN ORGANISATION

"I have a new CD coming out, and one of the songs is called *The Naked Bachelor*."
— ED JORDAN, POP STAR

"Just give me a chance, ladies. I am not as unattractive as I look."
— CHUNKO

FORTHCOMING TITLES BY
THE SAME AUTHOR

The Faked Chef

Separating the Wheat from the Chef, or Cooking Without Gluten

The Knackered Chef, or The Road-Runner's Cookbook

Too Many Indians, Not Enough Chefs – The Dilemma of Feeding the Third World

The Knickered Chef, or Catering for Cross-Dressers

The Naked and the Fed

The Knockered Chef, or My Life as a Transsexual Short-Order Cook

Yorkshire Pudding – A Brief Life of Cheffrey Boycott

The Nookied Chef, or Getting Lucky in the Kitchen

Playboy in the Kitchen – The Life and Times of Hugh Chefner

The Nicked Chef, or Shoot Straight, You Bastards

I Shot the Chef (but I did not use the recipe), or The Lost Recordings of Bob Marley

The Naked Chafe, or My Life Before Underwear

Rock of Ages, Chef for Me, or Cooking with Faith

Songs from Maurice Chefalier

Roman à chef

Harry Potroast – The Favourite Recipes of JK Rowling-Pin

Dr Chefago, or There's a New Sharif in Town

The **Naked** Bachelor

Your Essential Survival Guide to Modern Living

DARREL BRISTOW-BOVEY

Published in 2003 by New Holland Publishers (UK) Ltd
Garfield House, 86-88 Edgware Road
London W2 2EA
United Kingdom
London • Cape Town • Sydney • Auckland
www.newhollandpublishers.com

3 5 7 9 10 8 6 4 2

PUBLISHING MANAGER: Marlene Fryer
MANAGING EDITOR: Robert Plummer
EDITOR: Ronel Richter-Herbert
COVER AND TEXT DESIGNER: Natascha Adendorff
TYPESETTER: Natascha Adendorff

Set in 10,5 pt on 15,5 pt Melior

Printed and bound by Times Offset (M) Sdn Bhd

ISBN 1 84330 479 1

Contents

In lieu of free copies, this book is dedicated to the Bachelors who helped me:

Evan Milton

Ed Jordan

Rob and Gal

Chunko

Heather Dugmore

Samantha Manclark

Jann Turner

Sue de Groot

Leon the barman

Colonel Sanders

Jack Daniel

Peter Stuyvesant

Frankie

The Debonairs pizza deliverymen

Any errors and misrepresentations contained in this book are all their fault.

And to my godchild, whatever George and Nina decide to name it.

★ ★ ★ YOU MAY BE A WINNER! ★ ★ ★

Just buying this book makes you a winner in *our* book, but you may have won even more than our gratitude. The publishers of *The Naked Bachelor* have released a special unmarked limited edition containing paparazzi pictures of naked celebrities, printed on the blank end-pages in invisible ink.

Celebrities selected include Cameron Diaz, Helmut Lotti, Jane Fonda, Dick Cheney, the blonde in *Sex and the City* that isn't Sarah Jessica Parker, Bea Arthur, Morgan Freeman, an artist's impression of Nancy Drew, Janet Reno, Chelsea Clinton, a collage of the shapeliest *Pop Stars* winners from around the world and – in a special one-off fold-out feature – a group picture of the Baldwin brothers.

Have you bought a special edition copy? Special edition copies are outwardly indistinguishable from the regular edition, and the photographs can be made visible only by applying a low source of heat, such as a steam iron or heated signet ring, lightly to the surface of the paper. Try it now. If you have a special edition copy, you are a winner! Present your copy at your nearest bookseller and claim your grand prize: free takeaway pizza for a year from Debonairs ("Every discerning Bachelor's choice") and a hamper of Bachelor-related products. Included: one non-transferable voucher for a Saturday-night date with the bookshop cashier of your choice, and a free cellphone call-ring that plays a small, tinny version of the forthcoming single "The Naked Bachelor" by Ed Jordan.

intr
duc

The Bachelor is someone, married or not, who does not in his or her heart entirely understand **why** you would take a pizza out of a perfectly sound takeaway box and put it on a nice clean plate.

I DO NOT LIKE THE NAKED CHEF. IN FACT, I THINK I HATE THE Naked Chef. I'm sorry if that seems harsh, but it's true. Secretly, I believe all men hate the Naked Chef, no matter how many of his books we leave lying around the kitchen to impress female visitors.

Perhaps "hate" is a strong word. I am not saying I want to stalk Jamie Oliver and cause him personal harm – although he would be well advised not to find himself tooling down some dark country lane on that smart-alec scooter with me behind the wheel of an oncoming car. No, no, generally I wish him no malice. I would just like to have him expunged from all written and electronic records, and indeed from our collective memories. I'm serious. He is evil, is the Naked Chef. He is wicked (and I use the word "wicked" the way it is used in the dictionary and in the vocabularies of decent English-speaking adults, rather than the mouthy slang of oiks like the Naked Chef). Let me make this clear: the Naked Chef threatens our very existence. He must be stopped.

There are many reasons to dislike the Naked Chef. He is young, he is slim, he is rich and he is attractive to women all over the world. What's not to dislike? But worse: he makes the life of modern men a misery. Our womenfolk look at us with eyes that say, "Why can't you be more like the Naked Chef?" Well, the fact is that very few modern men are the Naked Chef. Most women have to make do with the Chef Who Only Wears Socks and a Ratty Towelling Robe Around the House, or the Chef Who Wears the Same Underwear Three Days in a Row. Some of us just don't look good naked. Others of us, let's be frank, aren't really even chefs at all.

It is not just that women find Jamie Oliver attractive. There have been many men over the years that women have found attractive. Mick Jagger, for instance, was unaccountably popular with the ladies. That was never a problem. No one seriously expected us to be like Mick Jagger. Deep in their hearts, most sensible women don't actually *want* to share a home with someone who might at any moment invite Keith Richards around for dinner, and who is in any case probably sleeping with their sister. But Jamie Oliver, despite a certain similarity in the lips department, is entirely different to Mick Jagger.

Jamie Oliver doesn't sell cookbooks, he sells an impossible dream of how life could be. Cute! Easy! Tasty! With shiny utensils and an endearing boyish speech impediment! And it's all a lie. That's not how life is. He torments men with the simpering vision of who we should be, and worse: he torments women with an impossible vision of who we could be. He is responsible for more female disgruntlement than *Cosmopolitan* magazine, more feminine disappointment than Dr Ernest Gräfenberg, celebrated discoverer of the G-spot and also, if memory serves, the Loch Ness monster and the lost city of Atlantis.

Well, I am here to say: No more! The Naked Chef is not a suitable role model. We cannot be like that. If we are to be honest, we don't *want* to be like that. It is time to throw off the tyranny of the Naked Chef. The modern world is more treacherous, more confusing than the world that taunts us on those poxy cooking shows, and it is more difficult to always find fresh ingredients.

The Naked Chef is called the Naked Chef for two reasons. Firstly, because it was a good way to pre-hype the TV series.

Prepare yourself for a rash of copycat DIY shows: The Naked Grouter, perhaps, or The Exhibitionist Electrician, or The Plumber With More Than Just The Top Of His Butt Showing.

Secondly, because the smarmy little git claims to strip down the process of cooking to its bare essentials. Well, sorry, but it just doesn't work that way.

Modern life is fundamentally shifty and tricky and filled with painful oil splatters and sharp implements that can cause ruinous injury when clumsily handled by naked men in the kitchen. The sensible person does not cook naked, damn it. Sensible people need protection and concealment and outfits that make them look more attractive than cruel nature intended. Fluorescent overhead kitchen lights can be mighty unkind to those without clothing. If cooking is a metaphor for life – and I think you will agree that it is – then the wise modern man and woman give careful thought to what they wear in the kitchen.

That is why I have written this book: to offer a guide – a set of recipes, if you will, and I hope you will – to enable decent modern folk to pick their way through the pitfalls and hazards of our perilous modern world. We are not the Naked Chef; we have more on our plates than sprigs of aromatic herbs and fillets of hake. There was a time – oh, years ago – when life was simple. All you had to do was chase a mammoth off a cliff, filch a burning twig from Zog from two caves down who has a knack with the flint, and then you would have all the time in the world to lounge around preparing dinner and doodling on the walls while the fire preheated to the right degree of blaze. Ah, happy days they were. Hairy, but happy.

Nowadays we have all sorts of other things to worry about. We have complicated rituals and customs and baffling social codes that change just when we are getting the hang of them. Civilisation has given us stress and SMS and the tricky dilemma of finding a date on a Saturday night without using a club. (True, many modern folk nowadays find dates on a Saturday night *at* a club, but we could argue all day about which version of clubbing is more socially beneficial.) Civilisation has given us these problems and challenges, but civilisation is not entirely cruel. As compensation, it gave us the restaurant.

This is a book for people – men, yes, and women too – who are not the Naked Chef. That is you, and all your friends and family too, whether they will admit it or not. Many people are still in denial about not being the Naked Chef, or about not being someone who will ever be married to the Naked Chef. If you love them, you will help them. Buy them their own copy of this book. If you don't love them that much, steal money from their wallet to buy them their own copy of this book.

Do not – and I cannot stress this enough – do not lend them your copy of this book. You wouldn't lend people your copies of the Naked Chef's books, would you? No, you would not. You want them close to hand, prominently displayed in your kitchen or your breakfast nook, to suggest to visitors that you are the kind of person who is so proficient at this difficult game called life that you have the time and energy and inclination to spend your evenings dicing leeks and experimenting with strips of ginger. So, too, let it be with this book. You will want to keep it visible – half-protruding from beneath a cushion on the sofa, perhaps, or serving as a handy drinks coaster – to let the world know that you – yes, you – are wise to its tricks. And that you are prepared to deal with the world in the best possible way – with as little fuss and effort and fancy-pantsing as is humanly possible.

This book, dear friends, dear fellow Bachelors, will show you that it is okay not to be the Naked Chef. We can follow the demands of our idle, self-serving, eminently sensible natures, and we can still be happy and successful and find a date on a Saturday night. This book will enable you to make the most of not being the Naked Chef. So come with me now. Stand close, that's right. Don't be afraid, we are none of us naked here. Take my hand. No, my hand. Ready? Here we go.

The Naked Bachelor

ACTUALLY, BEFORE WE GO ANYWHERE, THERE IS SOMETHING I should probably explain. Those of you who are reading these pages, rather than just flipping through them in the hope of seeing photographs of naked people performing elaborate visual puns with spatulas and fresh produce, will have noticed that on the previous page I addressed you as a Bachelor. "Dear fellow Bachelors," I said. It is right there in the last paragraph. Check for yourself, if you don't believe me.

Now you may be experiencing one of two reactions. "Hey," you might be saying, "how did he know I am a bachelor?" Or, just as likely, "Hey," you might be saying, "I'm not a bachelor." That is not the bachelor I mean. I am talking about the Bachelor. Not all unmarried men are Bachelors, and not all married women are not. Bachelorhood is a state of mind. I will explain what I mean and you can decide for yourself, but I am confident in my own mind that you are indeed a Bachelor. The best of us are, you know, and if you have read this far I think you can congratulate yourself on being among the best of us. Certainly, *I* think you're top-notch.

The bachelor has had much bad press over the years, and quite right too. Giovanni Casanova was a bachelor, and so for many years were Warren Beatty and Hugh Hefner and Bill Wyman and those critters from *Big Brother* and Heathcliff from *Wuthering Heights*. I believe Russell Crowe is still a bachelor. Nice guys all, in their way, with the obvious exception of those critters from *Big Brother*, and no doubt loads of fun for a hand of poker or a quick one down at the pub, but you wouldn't want to introduce any of them to your younger sister. Hitler was a bachelor, come to think of it, before a woman married him in time to save the world. Some historians hold that invading Russia was his big mistake, but each night before I go to bed I say a quiet prayer of thanks to Eva Braun.

On the other end of the scale, most of the Popes have been bachelors, and the Lone Ranger and Tonto, and Tintin and Captain Haddock. Noddy and Big Ears were bachelors, not that there's anything wrong with that. Asterix and Obelix were bachelors, although they were French, so it doesn't count. Perhaps the image of the bachelor has never quite recovered from Cliff Richard's creepy ditty "Bachelor Boy", still a firm favourite in boy-scout campfire singalongs the world over. My scoutmaster was especially fond of humming it as he adjusted my woggle and offered to take me behind the tents and teach me the occult arts of the sheepshank. No one has much good to say about anyone with "bachelor of arts" after his name either, now that I think about it.

But they are bachelors. The Bachelor is something subtly different. How can I explain what a Bachelor is?

The Bachelor is someone, married or not, who does not in his or her heart entirely understand why you would take a pizza out of a perfectly sound takeaway box and put it on a nice clean plate.

The Bachelor is someone who, on some profound personal level, does not believe that three married couples taking turns to have each other over for dinner on Friday nights necessarily makes for a completely satisfying social life.

The Bachelor is someone who thinks that an evening with friends playing board games would be fun *for a change.*

A Bachelor will very often stay for another drink, even though the dog should have been fed half an hour ago.

Bachelors, when in a restaurant, rarely add up the cost of ingredients in their pasta and say: "You know, if you made this at home it would only cost about 30 per cent of what they charge here! Even with the fancy cheese! Even less if you make double and freeze the leftovers and have them on the weekend!" For that matter, the Bachelor seldom knows off-hand the supermarket price of pesto.

Bachelors don't feel the need to take up golf or join a book club, just to be able to get out of the house every now and then.

A Bachelor, typically, does not actively look forward to the office Christmas party.

Being a Bachelor is not just about having a healthy scepticism of the redeeming qualities of housework and domestication. Bachelors have an occasional appreciation of some of the pleasures of being single, even if they would not themselves choose to be single again. Regardless of what non-Bachelors might think, the principal pleasures of being single are not sexual. The principal pleasure of singledom is laziness.

Bachelors occasionally think: "Oh, to hell with what I am supposed to do." They sometimes go on to think: "Why am I supposed to do that?" Some graduate to thinking: "Who even cares why I am supposed to do that?" Good for them. Laziness is one of our great redeeming qualities. It is not that lazy people do not do what they have to do; it is that they don't see why they should do the other things. Laziness is a form of sanity.

It is clear-headed laziness that strips away the unnecessary, and frees us up to tackle the important challenges in life, like Third World debt and boy bands and how to find a date on a Saturday night.

In my experience, modern women often make the best Bachelors. Some like to refer to them as Bachelorettes, but I think that is insulting. Bachelorette sounds like "laundrette". It sounds like a place you send Bachelors to get washed and fluffed and neatly folded. That's not a Bachelorette, that's a marriage.

There are many different degrees of Bachelordom. Not every one of us is a Bachelor *cum laude*, and the world would be in a sorry state if we were. But if there is even a small corner of your heart that has ever wanted to say, "Sod it. The kids can make their own dinner. I'm going ten-pin bowling," well, my dear, you are a Bachelor, and that's the way to stay.

If you are a married Bachelor, god bless you, but it is the way of the world that Bachelordom is most concentrated among those of us who, by reason of inclination, circumstance or hygiene, are in a state of singleness. There are worse states to be in: Missouri, for instance, or Tasmania. (Remember that: the next time you say to yourself, "It's a Saturday night and I am all alone," reply to yourself: "At least you are not in Hobart.")

Married folk and couples in stable, loving relationships (which are not necessarily the same thing) have a natural buffer against the nips and burrs of everyday urban living. Being married or being in a stable, loving relationship has its own drawbacks, of course – if your partner gets to the remote control first you sometimes have to watch *Ally McBeal*, for instance, and sooner or later they will force you to eat muesli.

Plus you have to be nice to their friends. But the very best reason for having a partner is that it cushions you from the hard edges and shifting sands of this cruel modern world.

Those of us who are single are most vulnerable to the confusions and insecurities of these uncouth times. None is immune, but it is we who feel it most keenly. It is the Bachelor, and especially the single Bachelor, who stands naked on the cliff edge of the modern world, staring into the abyss as cold, dark winds pluck at their wrists. Do not be afraid, my friends. Help is at hand. Whether you are single or coupled, male or female, I encourage you to use this slim book as the pilot light in the gas burner of your life. Do what this book says, and everything will be all right.

the bac
at h

My first tip when it comes to housework: hire someone to do it for you. Failing that, more **cunning** strategies are in order. We shall work through some together. But as we go, do not forget the first creed of the Bachelor: Housework never made anyone **happy**.

Housework

YOU MAY HAVE NOTICED, WHILE WATCHING THE NAKED CHEF playing fast and loose with egg-flippers and colanders and the rules of English syntax during that series they filmed in his own home, how all around him was perfectly clean and ordered. The melamine gleamed, the cushions were fluffed, the aluminium fairly trembled from a good hard brushing. The place was not merely spick, but it would take a hard judge not to affirm that it was span as well. Looking at that house, the heart grew heavy. *How pristine!* sighed the heavy heart. *What a joy to live there! How happy I could be! What works I could achieve!* Do not be deceived, my friends. There is reason for such cleanliness: the Naked Chef is evil.

Not only that, but he earns a lot of money, so he can afford to have someone come around every day with a large canvas bag of wire brushes and soft cloths and cleansing unctions, and make it all look shiny. That would in fact be my first tip when it comes to housework: hire someone to do it for you.

Failing that, more cunning strategies are in order. We shall work through some together. But as we go, do not forget the first creed of the Bachelor: Housework never made anyone happy. Say it after me: Housework never made anyone happy.

Now, I don't want to sound sexist – I never want to sound sexist, especially when I am saying something sexist – but men and women have a different relationship to housework. I am not saying that women *enjoy* housework, any more than men *enjoy*

The Bachelor at Home

having to drive around in circles when they're lost rather than stopping to ask for directions, but unlike men, women see a need for housework. Even left alone and to her own devices, a woman is likely to rinse out the coffee cup before making another cup of coffee. I am told that many women living alone own such items as sugar bowls and saucers. What's more, they use them.

This is not the way of your hardened male Bachelor (and what better kind of male Bachelor is there?). The male Bachelor living alone is one of nature's great pragmatists. Take a closer look at the careers of the philosophers and rational sceptics and I think you will find that they learnt their trade during their Bachelor years, living alone and asking: "If a carpet is vacuumed in the middle of an apartment, and no one comes to see it, has it really been vacuumed at all?"

It is this approach that has caused such mighty strides in the advance of Western rationalism. The Bachelor, faced with the entropic chaos of his home, is forced to question the assumptions upon which his system of knowledge is based.

The ontology of dust

For instance: what is dusting? Dusting is not cleaning. Dusting does not remove dust from your home. Dusting simply agitates and relocates it. Dusting is precisely the same drama, played small, that we are seeing in the Middle East. Do you want your skirting board to become a miniature Gaza Strip? We who do not learn from history are doomed to repeat it. At the moment your dust is relying on passive protest to make its position felt. You don't want to push it into violence.

Besides, what is dust anyway? Dust is not dirt. Dirt just sits there; sometimes it requires scrubbing. Dust, on the other hand, can be shifted with a few flutters of a bundle of ostrich feathers. Dirt, you might say, is precisely an undesirable domestic residue that *cannot* be dusted. Besides, dust is dusty, not dirty. So why, then, do we frown upon dust? I ask again: What is dust?

Dust, my friends, as the Good Book tells us (the Bible, not Delia Smith), is that from which we all arise, and that to which we all return. To struggle against dust is to struggle – oh, as Sisyphus struggled against the rock and the high, high hill – with our own destinies. That dust against which we fight is you and it is me and it is quite possibly our great-great-grandparents. To fight against dust is to battle the inevitable. Peace comes with acceptance. (Besides, that might be a speck of Mozart you are flicking away, or the late, great John Denver.)

So you can see the importance of clear thinking when approaching the question of housework. Housework is for the philosophically unrigorous.

Housework: a justification

For the male Bachelor, there is only one reason to do house-work: a woman is coming to visit. To put it in the philosophical terms with which, say, Ludwig Wittgenstein might be more comfortable: Housework has functionality, not intrinsic value. (Wouldn't you like a T-shirt that says that?) The functionality lies in the fact that if you manage to lure a potential partner to your home and you have approximated the effects of house-work, she is unlikely to run screaming from the room, clawing at her own flesh and crying "Unclean! Unclean!" in a strangled voice.

As a rule of thumb, the frequency with which your house needs to be cleaned is entirely dependent on your romantic schedule. You need to clean your house the day before you invite a young lady around for the first time. If you have cleaned well, she will be impressed and look at you with new eyes. She may even feel sufficiently comfortable to sit down on an item of furniture. Congratulations – you have done your job. From now on she can get to know the real you.

Here are some handy hints and tips to help you with your housework management:

HOUSEHOLD MANAGEMENT TIP #1: UNDERSTAND FEMALE PSYCHOLOGY

A woman does not expect you to have an impeccable home. She does not even *want* you to have an impeccable home. Only Jerry Seinfeld and Frasier's brother keep an impeccable home, and you do not want to resemble too closely either of those gentlemen. A woman expects a certain amount of slop and mess in a Bachelor. It comforts her. It reassures her that you are incomplete and endearingly helpless without her. And she takes it as final proof that you are not homosexual.

To attract a woman, make sure your home is her idea of a mess. In other words, clean up your home. A woman's idea of a mess is clutter. It is a used T-shirt crumpled on the floor, or one shoe in the bedroom and the other in the lounge. It may extend to an empty pizza box beside the bed, although you are pushing your luck. A champagne cork beneath the television is a nice touch. Women's idea of a mess is not our idea of a mess. Do not enlighten them – they will not understand. In the world of women, dirt has no place.

Men can live with dirt. We draw the line at food that has changed colour, say, and we would never dream of wearing the same socks three days in a row without thoroughly spraying them with deodorant, but for us cleanliness is just a state of a little less dirt.

Notes towards a theory of dirt

My friend Chunko has a theory about dirt. Where housekeeping takes some men philosophically, Chunko turns to science. "You know how when you don't wash and you don't use deodorant for a few days, you smell very bad?" he said.

I nodded. I did know. Chunko is forever experimenting with the boundaries of personal toxicity.

"Well," he continued, "you know how after a certain period of time you stop smelling bad, because your body's natural system of self-regulation has reasserted itself?"

I nodded again, but more slowly this time. I had an idea I knew where his theory was taking him.

"Well," mused Chunko, "it must be the same way with your house. Things get very dirty very quickly, because the world of dirt is struggling against the oppressive world of clean, but if you leave things be, equilibrium will be established. A stable biosystem will assert itself. Things will not get any more dirty. After all, how dirty can something get? After a certain point, any new dirt that comes along will be rubbing off the dirt that was there before."

"And will your house stop smelling bad?" I asked. Chunko ignored me.

"Because even when things are clean, they are not really clean," he continued. "They are just at a certain point on the straight-line continuum of dirt. There is a world of unfriendly invisible beasties to the left of that point, most of them far more harmful than the dirt you can see. We just happen to call that point 'clean'. But if we can train ourselves to choose a different point, further to the right on the straight-line continuum of dirt, and call that 'clean', then we can live in a state of cleanliness forever and yet not ever have to clean up again."

At this point he paused, and his eyes became faraway and moist. His face was lit with the fevered light of the visionary. "It would be …" his voice quavered, and he had to stop for a moment. "It would be heaven on earth."

Chunko's theory may or may not be valid, but it violates the Doctrine of Visible Dirt, hammered out at the Pan-Global Inter-Gender Congress of 1862 as a compromise to facilitate an uneasy housekeeping truce between men and women. The Doctrine of Visible Dirt is simple: if it's visible, it's dirt. If it's not visible, it doesn't count. Looking behind the fridge is cheating.

HOUSEHOLD MANAGEMENT TIP #2:
YOU ARE NOT A HANDYMAN

This is important to remember, if you wish to save your strength and emotional resources for the real challenges of modern life. Modern life has seen fit to confound us with dating and e-mail etiquette and Eminem, but it does offer slight compensations. One of the compensations is that there are people you can pay to come round and fix things. Make use of these people. Unless you live in a little house on a prairie, there is no need to be a handyman.

It is acceptable to change your own light bulbs, but you are advised to stop short of any act of home repair that requires tools not provided on a Swiss Army knife. Feel free to open tins of beans or clip your fingernails or remove small stones from the hooves of horses, but do not get ideas above your station. When your cistern breaks or your pipes become blocked, do not be fooled into believing that a real man fixes his own plumbing. Before you plumb, ask yourself: "Am I a plumber?" If you have to ask, the answer is no. Besides, do you think plumbers do their own plumbing? They do not. Plumbers make so much money they can afford to hire their own plumbers.

HOUSEHOLD MANAGEMENT TIP #3:
KEEP IN A STATE OF READINESS

As a single man living alone, you never know when fortune may knock. You want to keep your home in a state of battle-readiness, so that when the opportunity arises to invite a young lady around for a cocktail or to watch a National Geographic special on television, the requisite clean-up can be executed within a period not exceeding twenty-four hours. Using common sense in everyday life will minimise the work when the crunch comes.

CROCKERY JUST MAKES WASHING UP

If the takeaway container didn't leak while it was being delivered to your door, why change it now?

NEVER WASH A SAUCEPAN

On those occasions when you have seen fit to cook for yourself, do not consider washing the saucepan. The lingering taste of whatever you cooked last will add richness and depth to your next creation. If it doesn't taste good, then why did you cook it in the first place? But if it doesn't, there is a simple remedy: add more Tabasco.

CONSIDER DUST COVERS

This is one of Chunko's more inspired ideas. He is in the process of patenting the Wall-to-Wall Dust Cover™. It is, really, a large expanse of fabric, cut to precisely fit your living room, with a strategically located square hole to accommodate the television. There is sufficient cloth to drape over any furniture and bookcases you may own. With the Wall-to-Wall Dust Cover™ in place, the Bachelor can confidently strew the room with chicken bones, empty beer bottles, cigarette ash and human vomit, although if the Wall-to-Wall Dust Cover™ will be in place for a period exceeding four months, it is advisable to simultaneously use *two* Wall-to-Wall Dust Covers™. This prevents seepage.

When the time comes to clean up, the canny Bachelor simply moves the television set to one side, gathers up the corners of the Wall-to-Wall Dust Cover™, ties the corners in a knot, and carries the whole sorry bundle outside, where it can be left for collection or thrown over your neighbour's wall, according to your mood. Step inside, and voila! A lounge as good as new.

SAFEGUARD YOUR SHEETS

Here is another difference between men and women: women make their beds. Yes they do, and they expect men to do the same. For most women, the made bed is the very symbol of civilisation. It is the acme – nay, the quintessence – of all that we strive to be. It is the made bed, most women would agree, that sets us apart from the beasts of the field. Most women would no more leave their home with the bed unmade than men would leave a bar with their beer unfinished.

I don't know if ever a study has been made on the subject, but I am willing to bet that the percentage of condemned women who arose on their final morning on Death Row and did *not* make their bed before being led away is so small as to be statistically insignificant.

You may remember the scene in *Titanic*, after the ship hits the iceberg, in which Kate Winslet rushes back to her cabin to make sure she has squared the counterpane.

Do not even bother arguing with women about making the bed. We have all tried it, and we have all failed. Admittedly, there are some men who make their beds. Famously, Nelson

Mandela made his bed every morning on Robben Island, and continues to make his own bed today. Alas, there are not many of us who are Nelson Mandela.

If we are to be honest, very few men even see the absolute need for sheets, unless they are in the happy position of anticipating the need for something absorbent. But choose your battles wisely, men. You are not going to win this one. Cut down on laundry worries and bed-making concerns by never using your bedclothes when you are alone. Have your bed made once, by an expert, then every night stumble home drunk and fall asleep on top of the covers with your clothes still on. Voila! Your bedroom is permanently ready for inspection.

NEVER USE YOUR STOVE

I realise this may be slightly impractical advice, but it is the only way to ensure that your stove stays clean. If the inside of your stove becomes dirty, you are in trouble, because no man in the history of the world has ever figured out how to clean a stove. There are products on the market involving industrial foam and ultrasonic bombardment, but no man has ever successfully used these products. There was once, in the 1930s, a travelling carnival in the American Midwest, sometimes visiting the Eastern Seaboard, which boasted as its star sideshow an act in which a man demonstrated how to clean a stove. He called himself Stove Austin – The Man of Steel Wool – and he was a nationwide sensation in the giddy months before being exposed by a Philadelphia reporter as nothing more than the bearded lady moonlighting for extra money. No, I warn you, men: if your stove becomes dirty there is only one remedy. You will have to move.

DO NOT BE TOO THOROUGH

When the race to clean up is on, do not approach the task as a typical man does. The typical man stands in the middle of his lounge and rubs his hands together and says, "Right, if I'm going to do this, I'm going to do this properly. I will clean this place so thoroughly it will never dare get dirty again! I will clean this home as Stormin' Norman Schwarzkopf cleaned up the road to Kuwait City! No home in the history of homes has ever been as clean as this home shall be!"

The man will then spend the next day sanding down the undersides of doors, polishing curtain rings, wiping light bulbs with a damp cloth, dusting between the pages of books and using a toothpick to clean out the spaces between the buttons on the TV remote control. Oh, it can get mighty bad for a man cleaning up. How bad can it get? To what reaches of monomania might a man be driven? All the way, my friends. All the way. Once I myself, preparing for a first-time visit from a lady, started trying to clean the inside of my stove. Deeper I went, and deeper, into the very heart of an impenetrable sootiness. The rest of 1996 is a blank to me, but still I flinch at sudden movements and sometimes I find myself absent-mindedly sculpting strange shapes and patterns from my mashed potatoes.

DO NOT NEGLECT THE FINISHING TOUCHES

Perfuming the air with the slight fragrances of ammonia and aerosol wood polish will subliminally impress your date. "Whoever lives here," her chromosomes will murmur to her mating instincts, "is not afraid of cleaning." If you have no

wood polish, do not be tempted to spritz the air with insecti-
cide or spray-paint. She will notice the difference.

Cooking

COOKING IS A BIG DEAL IN MODERN SOCIETY. I SUPPOSE IT HAS always been a big deal, in its way. If there were no cooking, we would eat all our food raw, which means evolution would have made our jaws grow bigger and bigger, rather than smaller and more streamlined. Without cooking, we would all look like Celine Dion.

Cooking has other recommendations. If it weren't for cooking, the potato would be a very unwelcome side dish. The tapeworm would become a food group. Sushi wouldn't be half as sexy. Sushi, indeed, would be just another word for fish. No, cooking is good, as far as it goes. But of late cooking has become something more.

Cooking is trendy. Cooking is lifestyle. Cooking is the new rock 'n' roll. Some have suggested that cooking is the new sex. I suppose cooking has much in common with sex, if you really want to think about it. Some things that cooking and sex have in common:

- Preparation is important.
- The ingredients should be fresh.
- Make sure you preheat to just the right temperature.
- It is polite to wash your hands before you begin.
- No matter how careful you are, there is always some kind of mess to clean up afterwards.
- Cooking is best for two, a little more difficult for several, but a lot less pressure when it is only you.

Oh, we could go on forever. It could be worse. Sex could be the new cooking.

If you are someone who enjoys cooking, I salute you. There has to be someone to feed the rest of us. But for we who do not know one end of a caper from another, cooking has become a lifestyle choice causing a great deal of anxiety. With the rise of the celebrity chef and cooking channels and the whole brouhaha and hullabaloo about food preparation, we non-cooks are beginning to feel that there is something wrong with us. We are out of step with the way the world is walking.

We used to be able to congratulate ourselves that we at least maintain the natural balance. "Ah, well," we could say as we sat in the lounge drinking while other people peeled tomatoes, "if the broth is spoiled, no one can blame us." Nowadays there is no such thing as too many cooks. Non-cooks are subversives. Non-cooks are the new smokers. (Actually, a lot of us are still the old smokers, which gives us a good excuse to leave the kitchen while other people are cooking.)

We do not yet experience outright hostility – no one is throwing bricks through our windows with notes tied around them saying, "If you don't like the heat, get into the kitchen" or anything like that. At the moment they content themselves with pitying eyes and a tone of voice such as older sisters use on unmarried women in their thirties. But this is how victimisation starts: with an arched eyebrow and a meaningful silence.

In the face of such social pressure, many non-cooks are tempted to cave in. They buy books and order non-stick pans from infomercials and purchase aprons with humorous slogans, like "Don't blame me, I only cook here," or "If it weren't for this apron I'd be naked". Resist, my friends. Cooking is a fad; like all fads, this too shall pass. Remember fondues? Remember wall-to-wall carpeting? Remember feng shui and koi ponds and CB radios and seashells as decorative features? Remember Jane Fonda's home-aerobics videos? Remember Mickey Rourke? We out-waited all of these things, and they passed. Be strong again. Do not bow to fashion.

Gentlemen – do not be intimidated by seeing the Naked Chef whip up something tasty for his missus after work with the minimum of fuss and washing up. Do not wonder why he can do it and you cannot. Remember: *He is a chef.* That is all he *can* do, besides exercise the skill of speaking non-stop for half an hour with a vocabulary of only seventeen words and three slang expressions.

Ladies – do not feel you have to cook to be a complete woman. Seriously, you do not. The kind of man for whom cooking is a relationship deal-breaker is not the kind of man with whom you want to be. Remember: it never stops with cooking. Let him go marry his mother, if that's what he wants. Say to him: "Stop being such a mother-marrier." But you may want to invest the time you are saving by not cooking in perfecting other useful domestic skills. For instance, can you tie a cherry stem into a reef knot with your tongue? Just a suggestion.

Bachelor's tip box:
Your kitchen can do nothing a restaurant cannot do better.

It is however advisable to have at least one dish that you can cook, even under pressure, even when drunk. You will want to cook this during the all-important courtship stage. Do not say to your prospective partner: "This is the only dish I can cook." Say instead: "I always feel happy when I am cooking this dish", or "This dish reminds me of home. I am glad I am sharing it with you." Say this every time. By the time your prospective partner feels comfortable enough to say, "For crying out loud, can't you make something else for a change?" you will know you are already in a relationship.

Make sure your dish has the virtue of being versatile. Remember this: You will never, *never* have all the ingredients your recipe calls for. Even if you go out shopping with the express intention of buying every ingredient, you will forget one, or it will not be in stock, or you will later discover you picked up the wrong packet because you were inspecting an attractive stranger out of the corner of your eye. If your special dish is unthinkable without fresh strawberries or Japanese fugu fish, you are asking for trouble. You need a dish that can be approximately recreated with whatever happens to be left over from the last time you cooked anything. This is why pasta is very popular with Bachelor cooks.

Cooking is very much a matter of your own conscience. You know how far you are prepared to go. You know how far you are qualified to go. Be humble. If you exceed your limits, the heat from the kitchen will melt the wax that holds your wings together.

To assist further, I have compiled this brief list of helpful tips and hints, which you might want to post in a prominent place.

Inscribe them in the butter with a blunt pencil, perhaps, or spell them out on your fridge door with alphabetic fridge magnets.

Cooking tips for Bachelors

- Try to cook alone. If others do not see you cooking, it is easier for them to believe you know what you are doing. To remove someone from the kitchen while you are cooking, there is a time-honoured technique. Ask them to peel the garlic.

- When serving the dish, always say: "The secret is in using fresh ingredients."

- When serving the dish, try to restrain yourself from saying: "I hope you're hungry!"

- Tabasco is a food group.

- Always add wine.

- Victims of natural disasters and the inhabitants of under-developed nations are the only people who ever express happiness at seeing soya beans, and even they are only being polite.

- Serve bread by all means, but be wary of bread with too many nuts, husks and unidentifiable items of roughage. It is possible for bread to be too nourishing.

- Strategic additions to the sauce can create a rich and intriguing under-taste that no one can quite identify. Marmite, for instance, or Coca-Cola or Jack Daniel's Tennessee Whiskey or that vinegary stuff in a packet of olives. Used sparingly, the brine from a tin of tuna can be a taste sensation, especially if there is no other tuna in the sauce. A splash of Old Spice can transform a dish, but always allow it to reduce.

- Be aware that brown rice carries religious overtones.

- Be creative if you must, but bear in mind that people have been cooking and eating for many years, if not longer. If you are the first person to think of adding fresh lime juice to scalloped potatoes, understand that there must be a reason for this.

- A watched pot does eventually boil, but it is generally an anti-climax.

- Food cooks fastest when you are in the lounge, watching television.

- When you think the sauce needs another two or three minutes, stop cooking.

- Never start a food fight you are not confident you can win.

- A dish of white grapes may add pizzazz to a race-day hat, but it is not dessert.

- Never apologise for the meal. Contemporary cooking is like modern art. If they don't like it, it is because they don't get it.

the
back
outs

Perforce, we must
venture into the world,
and it is no picnic out there.
It is confusing, distressing,
filled with traps and
dead-ends and
sharp-toothed things.

I N THESE FRIGHTENING TIMES, ALMOST EVERYONE IS TEMPTED to spend time indoors, where it is safe and cosy and we do not have to worry about diseases or haircuts or whether other people like us. "Cocooning" is what Faith Popcorn calls it, as though any sensible person gives a hootenanny what Faith Popcorn calls anything. Nomenclature is clearly not a strength in the Popcorn clan.

And yet this is not a frivolous subject. Cocooners take their lives – yes, their very lives – in their hands. No matter what social horrors await beyond the front door, the outside world is safer than the perils of your own home. Home is where the frightening things happen. In the interests of your safety, I have gathered certain facts and statistics to illustrate my point. Use them well: I do not know many facts and statistics. I doubt there will be others.

You will probably die at home

Consider this, before you decide to have a long lie-in next weekend: every year in the USA more than 400 000 people suffer injuries involving beds, mattresses and pillows. Think about that for a moment. That is almost 2000 injuries a day involving soft objects wrapped in linen. We are not talking about sore backs or grazes on your elbows here – these are injuries requiring emergency hospital treatment.

Consider: every year more than 50 000 Americans are injured at home by pens, pencils and other desk accessories. How does this happen? I have myself spent many long hours at desks when I would have been grateful for almost any injury as a welcome diversion, but I have never managed to achieve actual bodily harm.

There are domestic perils everywhere. A 2001 report by the Department of Trade and Industry in the UK reveals a creeping trend. Apparently the tea cosy, that quintessentially comforting English oddity, is itself becoming a lurking source of dread. Incorrect use of the tea cosy was responsible for a staggering 40 emergency hospital treatments over the previous twelve-month period, and the future looks yet more ominous – cosy-related accidents have doubled since 1999. There is no point in seeking safety in the bathroom, though – more than 3000 people are hospitalised each year after falling over laundry baskets.

You never know whence danger will strike at home. Clogs, those unsightly but otherwise seemingly benign items of Dutch footwear, cause some 300 accidents a year among "people who wear them incorrectly" (on their heads, perhaps, or over their eyes while running downstairs), and they are closely followed by place mats (165 accidents per annum) and bread bins, a grow-ing menace at 91 serious injuries a year. How do you manage to be mangled by a bread bin? I don't know. Ask a Brit, if you can extricate him from the jaws of his place mat.

Personally, I would like to meet any of the several hundred English folk who last year reported serious injury as a result of a mishap with the ceiling. Anybody who has a run-in with the ceiling must have an interesting tale to tell.

I think I have made my point. For our own sake, we cannot spend all of our time at home. The longer we are at home, the greater the chance of some disabling mishap. Perforce, we must venture into the world, and it is no picnic out there. It is confusing, distressing, filled with traps and dead-ends and sharp-toothed things. Fear not, my friends. Like Scott of the Antarctic, I have suffered that you may prosper. I have ventured out into the world and I have braved hard times and cruel fortune in order to draw up maps and charts to guide us through the shoals and rocky shores. Unlike Scott of the Antarctic, I have returned to share them with you. More like Amundsen, I suppose, or Shackleton. Plus, I didn't have to eat any husky dogs. But in the modern world there are worse things to eat than husky dogs.

The Supermarket

SOONER OR LATER, WE ALL GO GROCERY SHOPPING. THERE ARE those who welcome the dawn of online grocery shopping with a to-your-door delivery service as a means of avoiding the gross humanity of the mall, but this is not a satisfactory solution. The plums are always bruised when they arrive, and the ice-cream has very often melted. Besides, it is a human need to feel an object before you buy it.

If you are anything like me, you need to shake the boxes and thoughtfully heft the jars in your hands so that you can assure yourself that you are choosing the best of all possible boxes and jars. *This* is the box with several more cornflakes than the rest. *This* jar contains the tastiest olives – and look! None of the pimentos have fallen out!

So, you will have to visit a supermarket. Be warned: supermarkets are weird. With the possible exception of group therapy sessions or flying economy class, there is nowhere else in the world that you will find yourself paying money for the experience of sharing so much of your intimate life with members of the general public.

Toilet paper

I have a friend named Victoria who will only buy triple-ply toilet paper. This is not in itself a bad thing, although there are those who argue that triple-ply is a false luxury. "All content, not enough form," says Chunko, when we allow him to air his opinion on the subject. But Victoria buys triple-ply because she is afraid of what people will think when they look at her trolley.

"I don't want them to think, 'What kind of a loser skimps on the toilet paper?'" says Victoria. "I don't want them to think, 'If she skimps on the toilet paper, where else does she skimp?' Only a person who doesn't much love herself would skimp on toilet paper. If you skimp on toilet paper, it's like saying: 'I am a drug addict!' or 'I sell my body to strange men in the afternoons!'"

"Is that what you think when you look at the toilet paper in other people's trolleys?" I asked.

"I don't really look at other people's trolleys," said Victoria.

I didn't ask any more, because frankly Victoria is a little weird on the subject of toilet paper. But then who isn't? Toilet paper is a symbol of some sort, although I am not entirely sure what. Certainly toilet paper is a puzzling consumer item.

For one thing, I don't understand printed toilet paper. Often in a supermarket my eye is drawn by a stack of toilet rolls with those strange green prints of flowers or paisley patterns or fractals. What is the thinking behind printed toilet paper? If ever there were a product of which it might truly be said that any measure of decoration is redundant, I would have thought toilet paper would be it. And pacemakers, I suppose. But especially toilet paper.

Do some people prefer patterned toilet paper? Really? *Really?* Why? Do they find it soothing? Do they think just the right pattern of toilet paper can really add class to a joint? Oh, of what fluff and vanity are we mortals made?

Some years ago – back in the 1980s when everybody thought they had an idea that would make them money – I recall a company launching a series of toilet-roll novels. Well-known works of literature, selected by inscrutable criteria, were to be printed on toilet rolls for the purpose of enlivening one's daily seclusion. It was an alarming thought. It gave horrible new meanings to the name "Reader's Digest", for one thing.

I spent years thinking, as one does, about appropriate books to be toilet-rolled. *The Lord of the Rings* would be a start, and if you had triple-ply you could get all three done at once, which is a mercy. I have always found Jack Kerouac to be an author of especially laxative talents, but I would also propose any of a number of randomly selected self-help books and motivational tracts. *Who Moved My Cheese?* is already rectangular-shaped toilet paper, if you want my opinion, and I would welcome the opportunity to have a new edition of a well-known relationship-advice book titled *Men are from Mars, Women are from Venus, and now they are both on Uranus*. There are others: I like the Sherlock Holmes stories, but who wouldn't relish an edition in which the great detective tells his sidekick, "It's alimentary, my dear Watson."

Now what started me on toilet paper? Oh yes, supermarkets. Be on your mettle in a supermarket.

Do not be intimidated

Male Bachelors experience frequent moments of panic in supermarkets. The razor blades are never where you found them last. Fear not! You do not have Alzheimer's. It is a strange game played by supermarket employees. They sit behind one-way glass, watching you trudge optimistically to men's toiletries, then the health and hygiene section, then the cigarette counter and check-out tills, all the while cackling: "Ho! Ho! The fool! He'll never think of looking under the frozen turkey drumsticks!" Do not panic if you cannot find the razor blades. Be Zen. Empty your mind. If you are meant to have them, sooner or later the razor blades will find you.

Female Bachelors report moments of insecurity in super-markets, especially those that stock a range of exotic deli products. "What am I supposed to do with a tin of Thai coconut milk?" they cry. "How do you use sun-dried mango? Are there really people in the world who know what to do with a jar of anchovy fish flakes?" Male Bachelors are less affected by ingredient anxiety. We just assume that we won't know what to do with anything that isn't mayonnaise or a piece of toast.

Ladies, do not be intimidated. No one buys those products. They have been there since 1973. When a newfangled foodstuff becomes fashionable, they just change the labels. Most of those tins contain ready-to-mix fondue dip. Those products are just there for show. The supermarket managers think they add class to the joint.

Food fashions are fickle. They change inscrutably overnight. We are all familiar with the story of the sun-dried tomato. The sun-dried tomato was the biggest Italian overnight success story since Don Vito Corleone, or perhaps the Renaissance. Before the 1980s, where was the sun-dried tomato? Languishing on some Sicilian coastline, that's where, making a humble living between anchovies and thick slices of crusty bread, dreaming dreams no bolder than a glass jar in the storefront of a Neapolitan trattoria.

Before the 1980s, if you said "sun-dried tomato", people thought you were talking about Brigitte Bardot.

Suddenly the sun-dried tomato was everywhere. The sun-dried tomato was the new hula hoop. It was the Rubik's cube. You couldn't move for sun-dried tomatoes. There were sun-dried tomatoes on pizzas and in omelettes and inside muffins. People slapped sun-dried tomato on French toast and called it Italian. Barmen in swanky Californian drinking holes made Bloody Marys from sun-dried tomatoes – they didn't quench a thirst, but they had a piquant aftertaste. The sun-dried tomato appeared on the cover of *Time*. It was the hour of the sun-dried tomato. The sun-dried tomato outshone the sun.

Where is it now? Oh, it's still around, making a decent enough living, but the glory days are over, and the salad days are far less frequent. The sun-dried tomato is the Nick Nolte of fashionable foods. But this is still a happy ending. Not all fashionable food stories end as well as the story of the sun-dried tomato. Let me ask you this, then I will say no more: Whatever happened to chicken *à la* king?

Supermarkets are not singles bars

There is an urban myth that supermarkets are good places to meet people. My friend Chunko believes this myth. "Sunday mornings at the supermarket," he says, "are the best times to meet that special someone."

"Have you ever met that special someone at the supermarket on a Sunday morning?" I ask him, but Chunko seldom answers inconvenient questions.

Chunko's reasoning is thus: not only is it easier to identify a single woman in a supermarket on a Sunday morning than it is in a club, but you yourself are displayed to best advantage. If you are grocery shopping on a Sunday morning, you can't help but appear responsible, mature and – unless she catches you comparison-shopping for toilet paper – intriguing.

People imagine that it is easier to use an approach line in a supermarket than it is in a club. This may or may not be true. If you are going to approach someone, stick to something simple, like: "Could you tell me where the frozen fish fingers are, please?" Avoid any line you may have heard in a porno-graphic movie, or any line that your friends think would be a really good approach line in a supermarket. Ladies, I'm talking to you too.

Some approach lines to avoid:

- "Excuse me, ma'am, do you know where the extra-sized condoms are kept?"

- "Excuse me, sir, but can you tell me if these melons are ripe?"

- "Oh, look, we're walking up the aisle together!"

- "I notice you are considering buying those avocados. Did you know that the word 'avocado' is derived from the Spanish word *aguacate*, which is in turn derived from the Aztec word *ahuacatl*, meaning 'testicle'?"

- "I don't believe in sell-by dates."

- "Say, did you shoplift a tin of peaches, or are you just pleased to see me?"

- "Good music, huh?"

- "What's the deal with printed toilet paper, anyway?"

The Hairdresser

U NLESS YOU ARE DAVID BECKHAM – AND I WOULD LAY MONEY that you are not, unless the UK edition of this book has very large print and many brightly coloured pictures – you will need to leave your home to have your hair cut.

It is important to have your hair cut. People with bad hair have it hard in this world. They seldom have decent jobs – unless you consider running a website to be a decent job – and they frequently end up on *The Jerry Springer Show*. You may think it is not so bad to be on *The Jerry Springer Show* – for one thing, everyone on *The Jerry Springer Show* seems to have more sex than we do – but ask yourself: "Do I want to have sex with a toothless blood relative?" Well? Do you? Have a haircut already.

Hairdressers can be scary. Some men of my acquaintance still prefer old-fashioned barber shops. They are cheap and traditional and, well, more masculine. All this is true, but it will be no consolation when you have a haircut like Kevin Costner's. It is a simple rule of modern living: Never have your hair cut by a heterosexual man.

A visit to the hairdresser's salon is fraught with anxiety. There are unseen codes and conventions, and most of what happens is designed to make you feel insecure and ill at ease. That is what people pay for nowadays: if we feel insecure and ill at ease, we know we're getting our money's worth.

Here are some tips for visiting the hairdresser:

CONSIDER THE NAME OF YOUR SALON

Besides headline writers in the sports section of the daily newspaper, hairdressers are the last custodians of the pun. There is scarcely a city in the world without a Streaks Ahead, a Step Ahead, a Beyond the Fringe, a Curl Up and Dye, a Chitty Chitty Bang Bang, a Hair Jordan, a La Cage Aux Follicle, an I'm Not Drowning, I'm Blowing and Waving. I leave it to you whether you consider atrocious puns to be reassuring indicators of the aesthetic sensibilities of the establishment in whose hands you are placing your personal appearance. Just think about it. That's all I'm saying.

MAKE CONVERSATION

Hairdressers become resentful when you avoid conversation. Hairdressers spend fully one-third of their tuition at hairdresser school on a module called Making Conversation. They learn such questions as "So, how is work?" and "So, what line of work are you in?" and "You know we had one of those *Big Brother* housemates in the other day. She's really very down-to-earth."

If you do not respond, hairdressers become resentful. They think, "What a waste of a perfectly good education." They think, "Well, if *he* can't be bothered, then why should I listen to anything he says?" Do not shrug like that; they will apply this reasoning to statements like: "Not too much off around the ears, please."

If you are pretending to read the newspaper to avoid conversation, do not omit to steal frequent glances in the mirror. Of course, this will not help. If at any point you are unhappy with your haircut, if you think "Say, that's not what I asked for at all," it is already too late. If you point at your head and start gurgling, "But … but …", a certain gleam will enter your hairdresser's eyes. Your hairdresser will say one of three things:

1) "Trust me, you're going to love it."
2) "If I stop now it will be uneven."
3) "So, what line of work are you in?"

At this point, make conversation. It will minimise the damage.

PREPARE YOURSELF FOR LOSS

Hairdressers are like romantic partners. You spend your life searching for one who listens and understands and helps you be the best you that you can be. When you find them, you hold your breath, waiting for them to leave. I have lost more hairdressers than I have romantic partners, and the long-term damage is worse.

Hairdressers are skittish. Scarcely have I found someone I can trust, when he or she packs up clippers and goes to work on a Mediterranean cruise ship. One went to Ghana to be a missionary. One just died. They never leave a forwarding address. Hairdressers are modern-day gypsies, except gypsies skip the neighbourhood with your silverware and your youngest daughter. When good hairdressers leave, they take something far more precious.

If you want to keep a hairdresser, play it cool. Don't let them know how much you need them. Do not call the next day to tell them how much you are enjoying your cut. If you must call, wait at least three days. If you can, leave a message.

Do not hang on their every word when you are in the chair. Smile cryptically. Absent-mindedly forget their name. Casually ask questions about the new hairdresser in the salon. Do not say things like: "I don't know what I would do without you" or "I dreamt about you the other night." Rather say things like: "You know, maybe I should start wearing a hat." Never let them take you for granted.

Flying

11 SEPTEMBER 2001 CAST LONG SHADOWS. IN ITS WAKE, many people adjusted their values and made appropriate resolutions. I know I did. I resolved never to fly economy class again. When I go, I'm going out with enough leg-room. When my last order is called, I am going to be sipping champagne from real glasses, not those little plastic beakers that slop your fizzy cooldrink each time you fly over a bump. I am going to meet my Maker with an unlimited supply of moist towelettes.

No sir, I don't fancy dying in economy class. How would they separate the body parts for identification purposes? You can scarcely separate body parts in economy class *before* the plane has crashed. I don't want my teeth to be scraped up and buried in an urn with the hipbone of the fat sales rep sitting next to me. And he always is sitting next to me, that guy. When I go, I want to be surrounded by a better class of person than you meet in economy class.

I suppose I am hoping that a seat in front of the blue curtain will change my luck. You see, I have a dream.

The dream of the flying Bachelor

Some dreams take longer to die than others. In my time, I have pretty much figured out which dreams to jettison. I've just about accepted that Frank Sinatra will not invite me to join the Rat

Pack, for instance, and the chances are looking increasingly remote that I shall be appointed as the third Hardy Boy.

Still, there are some dreams I just cannot shake. Beating up Jamie Oliver, say. And then beating him up a second time. And the biggest of all: every time I board a commercial airliner, I cannot stop turning my mind to the glorious possibility that this time, oh please, *this time* I will be seated beside an attractive stranger.

Is it so much to ask? I have downgraded the dream over the years, for fear of being too demanding. In my younger days I imagined the attractive stranger would transform my life. We would fall in love before the seatbelt lights had been extinguished, and we would leave our old lives to live and love together. On the anniversary of our meeting each year we would fly somewhere exotic and far and hold hands as the plane took off.

As I grew older, I just hoped for sex in the bathroom, or perhaps a little how-do-you-do under the blanket. ("If we crash in the Andes and have to eat each other," she would say in a sultry half-whisper as the cabin lights dimmed, "you can start with me.")

But I am even older now, and the dream is more modest. I just want to sit next to someone attractive on an aeroplane.

It hasn't happened yet. Attractive people all fly on a different airline. I don't know which airline it is, and the attractive people aren't saying. If the marketing people for that airline knew their business, they would build it into their ad campaigns. "Fair hair? Dark hair? Good bone structure?" the ads would go. "We've got 'em! Fly Attractive Air, where all seats are in first class!"

Every so often, I have in fact seen an attractive person approaching up the aisle, looking for their seat. They obviously wandered onto the wrong shuttle bus, but they are determined to make the most of it. They draw nearer and nearer, and their eyes seem to move to my row. *Yes!* I gasp silently, pretending to read the laminated safety instructions. *Yes! Good things come to those with faith! Oh, happy day!*

And each time that attractive person just passes on by, like the moon coming briefly from behind the silvered clouds on a summer's night, and as they pass, all the universe softly sighs at once. Ah, but do not weep for me, my friends. I still have my dreams.

Bad company

It's all very well for people in stable, loving relationships. They bring their own seat-partners with them, and if their seat-partners are not attractive, well, whose fault is that? It is the rest of us who are at the mercy of budget-traveller demographics.

There are many types of undesirable travelling companions. Fat sales reps are bad, of course, but they are preferable to babies. I don't care for babies. They are noisy and they smell bad and they all look the same and they wear their bodily fluids on the outside. But why am I telling you this? You have seen babies before. You may even have one of your own, in which case you were probably sitting behind me the last time I was on an aeroplane. I believe aircraft should be divided into three classes: Business, Economy and Infant. My proposals are still tentative, but at present I conceive of Infant Class as a lead-lined canister somewhere in the hold.

I become irate when I am told that I cannot bring a second piece of hand-baggage onto the plane with me. The last time it happened, I pointed at some Russian-looking woman brushing wisps of hair out of her face. Women carrying babies onto airliners always look Russian to me. I don't know why.

"But look at her!" I complained. "*She's* carrying two pieces of luggage!"

"One of those is a baby, sir," said the steward firmly.

"But my hand-baggage isn't going to yowl and discharge liquids!" I yelled. "It will just sit there under my seat! No one will even know it's there! Tell me true – wouldn't you rather have my stylish hand-valise with retractable handle on your plane than that squirming mass of barely differentiated epithelial cells?"

But, as you will know if you have ever raged against the monstrous regimen of infants, it was to no avail. And I couldn't even defend myself by lighting up a cigarette. That's what cigarette regulations are for! To make public spaces more baby-friendly! It's an outrage. The only reason I took up smoking in the first place is that I once read a warning label that said: "Caution: smoking is harmful to babies". *Ho!* I thought. *My path is clear! All I need is a brisk nicotine habit and no decent mother will bring her joyous bundle near me again. My life will be shorter but infinitely more elegant.*

Still, there is this to say about babies in the seat beside you: they seldom try to make conversation. Or, if they do, they are easy to discourage. Making a scary face usually works. If they are a little older, you may have to shake a fist at them or stab their teddy bear with your plastic cutlery set. Alas, these measures rarely work with adults.

I don't know why certain people feel obliged to make conversation on an aircraft. They are the same people who get into a crowded elevator and say aloud, as though for the first time, "Isn't it funny how everyone in lifts always looks at the floor numbers?" They seem to think this will draw your eyes away from the floor numbers. Perhaps they think it will elicit a friendly chuckle, an instant of shared recognition that, after all, we are all just human beings together. Not with me, mate. If you want human contact, go to a massage parlour.

Unfortunately, on an aeroplane – especially those long-haul international flights – it is difficult to keep staring at the illuminated seat numbers for the full duration of the journey. Sooner or later your concentration will waver or your neck will go into spasm. More cunning stratagems are required.

Discourage conversation

Beware the moment when the person beside you says, "So, are you travelling on business?" It is important that you do not give a straight reply. If you do, they will take it as an invitation to discuss their daughter's wedding, for which they are flying to London. The woman beside me is always flying to London to attend her daughter's wedding. This is true even if the flight is not going to London. I don't know how that happens.

No, you must use guile. Old-school travellers pretend to fall spontaneously into a deep sleep. This can be effective, although it is surprisingly tiring to feign sleep for twelve hours. Feigned sleep is always more convincing than actual sleep. The moment your breathing becomes less theatrically deep and rhythmic –

The Bachelor Outside

like, say, when you actually do fall asleep – the person beside you will press their teaspoon into your ribs and say loudly, "Oh, you're awake! Did you sleep well?" Plus you will miss loading up on free booze.

Some recommend pretending to know no English, or simulating an epileptic fit, or vomiting into your shoes, but these too are difficult acts to sustain. No, the only effective remedy is to persuade the person beside you that *they* do not want to speak to *you*.

My friend Chunko subscribes to this principle. He always carries a German pornographic magazine of unspeakable vileness, titled *Das Bladder*. "No one would make conversation with a man reading *Das Bladder*," he declares confidently. On the whole I expect he is right, but personally I wouldn't want to run the risk of bumping into the person who *does* want to make conversation with a man reading *Das Bladder*.

Here's what works for me: spread across your tray-table a collection of medical pamphlets emblazoned with the words "Contagious Airborne Diseases – A User's Guide". Study these pamphlets, pausing at intervals to frown and take your pulse and mop your brow. Turn to your neighbour and say, in a strangled voice, "Do I look mottled to you?" Cough piteously into a small, sodden handkerchief. Unless your neighbour is a specialist in contagious airborne diseases, which is unlikely in economy class, you should have an uninterrupted flight.

Dinner Parties

ANY SELF-RESPECTING DINNER PARTY NEEDS A BACHELOR. Bachelors are decorative and fun and they brighten a room. Plus, Bachelors make good conversation. They know that if they make good conversation, they will be excused from having to reciprocate with dinner parties of their own.

Dinner parties without Bachelors are bad dinner parties. Bad dinner parties are God's way of telling us that He does exist, but He does not like us. Time at a bad dinner party warps and woofs and folds upon itself, like the special effects in an old episode of *Star Trek* in which the time-space continuum slowly fills with molasses. Have you seen that episode? No? Oh, well.

My idea of hell is to spend forever in a bad dinner party that never ends, with the hostess pouting and saying, "Aw, you didn't like the cauliflower!" and the host leaning back in his chair and saying, "So, we're thinking of making renovations to the house." Or, worse: "Somebody e-mailed me this really funny joke the other day ..."

These are things that happen when people throw bad dinner parties. Most dinner parties are not so much thrown as allowed to slip loosely from the hands and fall to the floor with a plop, but bad dinner parties should be firmly seized and hurled through an open window, as you would hurl Robbie Williams if he arrived to collect your daughter for a date.

And yet still we agree to go to dinner parties. There is some part of us that half-expects a dinner party such as you see in old movies. Ah, the dance of easy wit and limber repartee! Ah, the stories lightly told, the crackle of conversation, the smooth feint and thrust and parry of playful flirtation over the sorbet! It is seldom like that. Sure, you might have a few laughs after the wine takes effect and end up singing old eighties songs with dessert, but most often dinner parties are just a more boring version of staying at home.

The only good reason for a dinner party is the conversation, and that is half the trouble. For years I was convinced that I am the Jonah – or do I mean the Ishmael? No, I'm pretty sure I mean the Jonah – of conversation. I was aware that there were such things as good conversations, and I was led to believe that people around me were having them, but they never seemed to be happening anywhere I was. What sex was for me as a teenager, good conversations were when I became an adult. (Sex too, to be honest, but sometimes it's better not to be honest.)

I would find myself in a discussion about the cost of real estate, or about the sporty features of the new Mini, and I would think to myself: "I am the black cat of conversation. I am the ladder under which conversations wander. If I weren't here, these people would be talking about something interesting."

It was only recently that I began to wonder if perhaps it is not entirely my fault. Maybe – just maybe – people don't know how to talk any more. Certainly they don't know how to listen. Even Oscar Wilde wouldn't cut much mustard at today's dinner party. Try it for yourself: pick a conversational quote from Oscar Wilde (oh, go on, do: no one in your circle is going to recognise it). Wait for the right moment, then say in a voice clear and dry: "The only difference between a caprice and a lifelong passion is …" You will get no further. The brunette at the bottom of the table will interrupt to tell her neighbour in a voice like a paper bag being crumpled about the Thai restaurant across town she went to last Saturday.

To be fair, it wouldn't be a picnic to actually have Oscar Wilde at your dinner party, and not just because he would eat all the potatoes. The great conversationalists of yore were really monologists. For them the opposite of speaking wasn't listening, it was waiting, but no one even waits nowadays. When they're not tripping over themselves to spill the kind of conversation that clatters to the ground and rolls about like loose change, they are volunteering the unwonted and unwanted information that in more civilised societies would have them tied in a sack and dropped in a river. I was recently at a cocktail party at which a stranger wandered up, clutching a Heineken. She said to me, and I am not making this up: "You know, I shouldn't drink beer. It's the very worst thing for a yeast infection."

How would you respond? What would David Niven have said? Would he have launched nervously into an anecdote about a porn actress he'd once met named Candida Camera? Further proof, if proof were needed, that I am not David Niven. That is the tragedy of being a poor conversationalist at a party – you are like an iceberg drifting toward the equator. Not only do you diminish yourself with each passing moment, but you sink those with whom you come in contact.

Are you unsure whether or not you are a poor conversationalist? Ask yourself: "Have I in the past month discussed the crime rate, the exchange rate, motor cars, my gym routine? Have I told an anecdote involving my children, or the last time I was in London? Above all, have I told a joke at the dinner table?"

There is nothing worse than people who tell jokes. I see no difference between someone telling me a joke, and someone reciting me a poem they have written. They both arouse in me the desire to stick my head in the oven, where I cannot hear them.

(Remember the Bachelor's creed: The only excuse for telling people you write poetry is if you died tragically young many years ago.)

But fear not, gentle reader. As ever, I have suffered that you may thrive. Herewith please find the Naked Bachelor's guide to improving your conversation. The list is not exhaustive. Let the same be said about your conversation.

- Just because it happened, doesn't make it interesting.

- Great people talk about ideas; average people talk about things; small people talk about the food.

- If your sexual fantasies were of the slightest interest to other people, they wouldn't still be fantasies.

- Think before you speak. Read before you think. Wash your hands before you read.

- Do not flatter yourself you are having an original thought. Original thought is like original sin. It happened a long time ago, to someone else.

- Only a cad says everything he means, and only a bore means everything he says.

- Unless you are Joseph in the court of Pharaoh, or Dorothy in *The Wizard of Oz* – and I would venture to suggest that you are not – that unusual dream you had last Tuesday is of interest to precisely no one.

- This is not a good time to overcome your inhibitions.

- Gossip is only really interesting when it is about you.

- Never apologise. Rudeness is forgiven; cowardice never.

- If you have to tell jokes to be funny, you aren't.

And most importantly: Always leave the party five minutes before you run out of things to say.

Bachelor's tip box:
There is no way to respond politely when the host suggests a game of Pictionary after dinner. Do not even try. Simply strike him and leave.

Weddings

CONTRARY TO THE FERVENT HOPES OF THE HIPPIES AND THE radical feminists and the communists, people still get married and they still have weddings. I suppose that is something to be said for weddings. Any institution simultaneously loathed by hippies and radical feminists and communists can't be all bad.

Weddings are difficult for single people. Mind you, weddings are not much fun for anyone else either. No one actively enjoys weddings, except tuxedo-rental outlets and confetti moguls and the young kids who get to take their first sneaky sips of alcohol when their parents aren't watching.

Even the cummerbund industry is finding little to cheer about in weddings nowadays. If it weren't for matric dances, the streets would be lined with cummerbund manufacturers holding up cardboard signs and rattling polystyrene cups.

Weddings pose more questions than they answer. For one thing, I've never understood throwing rice.

Under what circumstances did it seem a good idea to pelt the newly-weds with a staple Oriental food source? Which diabolical marketing mind at the Rice Board came up with that scheme? ("Okay, gentlemen, those sly buggers at De Beers have cornered the wedding jewellery market, so we'll have to shelve the rice-on-a-chain range for now. But I have another idea – this may seem far-out at first, but hear me through …") What do they throw at weddings in China? Baked potatoes?

Side salads? Come to that, what do they throw at weddings in northern Ethiopia or rural Zimbabwe? Stones? But forget rice. Bachelor parties are just as puzzling.

The Bachelor Party

I don't like bachelor parties. Escorting a grown man in a nappy from pub to pub and buying him drinks is not my idea of fun. It feels too much like being friends with Ronald Reagan. Even worse are those creep-fests where a bunch of guys sit in a room and drink beer and wait for a stripper to arrive. Call it what you like, but I don't feel entirely at ease in the company of seven men with erections. I'm sorry, but that's just the way it is. I could try to phrase it more delicately, but that is what it comes down to. At a certain stage of the evening, you look around and you think: "Hey, I'm in a room with seven men with erections." And that's just not nice.

Worse still are those so-called "new man" bachelor parties, where you all go climb a mountain or walk in the woods and hug each other and affirm your manhood and beat your tom-toms. Even worse, you take turns to beat each other's tom-toms. There are men with cable-knit jerseys and neatly tended beards that make a living out of running these new-man bachelor party jerkathons. They call them "premarital transition rituals". I'm not kidding, but I wish I were. For god's sake, men, get a grip, and I don't mean on each other.

Go to bachelor parties if you must, but remember this: the people who most enjoy bachelor parties always seem to be married men. That is something to think about.

Choose your wedding well

Do not attend every wedding to which you are invited. No one can hear that many renditions of Celine Dion's "My Heart Will Go On" and hope to escape without lasting injury. Be selective. Weddings to avoid:

- **Any wedding in which the happy couple have written their own vows.** The personal touch may make for a good marriage, but it generally results in a wedding ceremony to make even the angels on high snigger and roll their eyes and nudge each other in the ribs. Most people can scarcely be trusted to write a note for the milkman, let alone wedding vows. I once attended a wedding in which the groom gave liturgical vent to his enthusiasm for the love ballads of Phil Collins. Gentlemen, please: whether or not you really do have a groovy kind of love is not in my provenance to judge, but save it for the shower. Likewise, vows that include any part of the poetry of Kahlil Gibran are grounds for annulment.

- **Any wedding taking place in a quirky location.** Wedding locations are like sexual positions: they have all been done before, probably several times, and there are photographs to prove it. The fact that certain options are so rarely exercised should not be an encouragement – it should be a warning. Perhaps the only places where we can be certain that a wedding has not taken place are under my bed and in outer space. You can forget about coming over and crawling under my bed, I can tell you. Let me also counsel against outer space while I am about it. What good can come of it?

The confetti would float into the sensitive space rocket machinery, the bubbles in the champagne won't know which way's up, and all your guests will have names like Yuri and Tomsk. Besides, you want your wedding to have atmosphere.

- **Any wedding with a "character" conducting the ceremony.** Father Schmuley, the wisecracking lay preacher, who starts every ceremony with the words "Dearly beloved, and friends of the groom …", is not a suitable candidate to read your nuptials. Nor is Wise Man Pete, the guitar-strumming medicine man. And any couple being married by the Reverend Sun Myung Moon shouldn't expect to be able to keep their wedding gifts for very long.

- **Your own.**

Wedding gifts

Wedding gifts are troublesome. If people need to be given household appliances, they are not in a financial position to be marrying in the first place. And I refuse to buy gifts off wedding registers. People who post wedding registers always list the most expensive items so that they can return them and get lots of money. This practice should not be encouraged. And remember: no one was ever truly grateful for "something I made myself, with love".

Do what I do: bring an empty gift-wrapped cardboard box with no label and add it to the pile. When no one is looking, remove the labels from all the other gifts.

(While rooting around the pile removing labels, should you happen to recognise a gift-wrapped satellite dish, say – and it is difficult to miss a gift-wrapped satellite dish – do not omit to telephone after the wedding and say, "So, did you like the satellite dish?")

Being the bride

I have no experience in being the bride at a wedding, but seventeen former brides filled in my questionnaire, and this is their advice:

• Valium.

Being the groom

A poll of my married male friends reveals a wider range of advice:

• Alcohol.
• Extra Valium for the wife.
• Do not steal any part of your speech from a wedding scene in a Hugh Grant movie.
• Do not push your bride's face into the wedding cake. It is not even funny when other people do it.
• Unless you really are Greek, do not joyously break the crockery. It does not make you look exotic and wild at heart. It just annoys the father of the bride, who will have to pay for it.
• At the reception, do not get drunk and dance the funky chicken. That is the job of the father of the bride.
• Do not begin your speech with the words, "I see there are many beautiful women here tonight. Where were you when

I needed you?" Your bride may laugh, but she will never forget.

- Elope.

Being a guest

Weddings are not about sharing your special day with loved ones. Weddings are about saying, "Look at us, we're getting married. Don't we look good?"

Wedding etiquette is very firm about the polite response. The polite response is any response that implies deep envy and resentment. Your polite response can be accomplished in any number of ways:

- Weeping. Weeping is very polite at weddings. Weeping makes people think you are so envious you cannot help but sob at your own sorry state.
- Gossiping. It is very polite to murmur at a wedding about pre-marital quarrels, or financial troubles, or drinking problems. This makes you seem even more envious than the weeping guests. If you really want to be polite, say confidentially: "Oh, I *do* hope they will be happy, despite it all."
- Getting drunk.

Being the Best Man

In the past the principal role of the Best Man was clearly defined: to sleep with one or more of the bridesmaids. This was polite wedding behaviour. A Best Man who did not attempt to dishonour a bridesmaid behind the marquee was the subject of terrible whispers and rumours. But in recent years has arisen the appalling and frankly impolite fashion for appointing small female relatives as bridesmaids. At the last wedding at which I was Best Man, the bridesmaids were seven and nine years old. This presents a tricky point of etiquette. Fortunately, given the looseness of modern etiquette, bridesmaids may be substituted with unmarried aunts of the bride, with little lasting disgrace.

Bachelor's tip box:
In today's economic climate, the cut-off point for the free bar is getting earlier and earlier.

the
back in

We should all be in love. Love makes the world go round. Sometimes it makes the world go pear-shaped, but mostly it goes round. Whether we are single or coupled, gay, straight or a Big Brother housemate, love is **good**. Even the memory of it is good after it has gone.

AH, LOVE! AMORE! THE STUFF THAT – AS THE BRITISH POP band Wet! Wet! Wet! once reminded us – is all around us. That sensation very similar – as the Italian-American crooner Dean Martin firmly made the point – to the moon hitting your eye like a big pizza pie.

And he is right, you know. I was once hit in the eye with a big pizza pie. Fortunately there were no anchovies on the pizza – you might not think it, but anchovies sting like all blazes, and they cause the eye to become all red and weepy. Even without anchovies, being hit in the eye with a big pizza pie is a bewildering experience. You become disoriented and the cheese stains your collar. Once you have been hit in the eye with a big pizza pie, you tend to stagger around blindly while a thousand confused thoughts whirl through your mind: "Where did that come from?" and "Ow, my eye!" and "Thank god it's thin-based" and "Hmm, is that salami?" You are outraged and vulnerable and hungry, all at the same time. So you see, love really is like being hit in the eye with a big pizza pie.

We should all be in love. Love is, well, lovely. Love doesn't actually cause the crickets to crick and the buds to bud and soft winds to whisper through the cornfields, but it helps you appreciate it when they do. I am not one of those wretched cynics with big-screen televisions and large DVD collections who have given up on love. I believe in love. I welcome love. I greet love at the door with a hearty handshake and a brimming glass and I say, "Come on in, I've been waiting for you! Stay as long as you like. No, no. I insist. You take the bed, I'm perfectly happy on the sofa."

I sniff at the cynics who say: "Love never lasts." They are missing the point. Of course love doesn't last – it is like life, that way. Like life, love is always shorter than we anticipate, and more expensive, and it often has an inappropriate soundtrack. But, also like life, love is preferable to the alternative.

But love is a peculiar commodity. Like a sumo wrestler or a butterfly not yet dead, it is hard to pin down. If you were a futures trader, you would probably want to avoid the love futures. Or maybe you wouldn't. Don't ask me, I know nothing about futures trading. I do know this about love though: love is as undemocratic as money – it clusters around those who have more than enough of it already.

Whether you are single or coupled, gay, straight or a *Big Brother* housemate, love is good. Even the memory of it is good after it has gone. But love is sneaky. Like a Japanese kamikaze squadron, it attacks out of the sun. The wise Bachelor keeps himself or herself in a state of battle-alert.

Flirting

FLIRTING IS AN IMPORTANT LIFE SKILL – NAY, IT IS AN ART, AND as with all arts it exists to make life bearable. It adds sparkle to your day, pep to your stride. Unexpected flirting is like a shot of tequila, except that afterwards it doesn't cause you to shudder and make an unattractive face. At least, not if you've done it right. Flirting need not lead to anything – usually it is not intended to. It is simply a slight dance to distant music, a tippy-toe *pas de deux* of playful possibility.

I, alas, am a poor flirter. When I try to flirt, I think so much about what I should have just done that I forget what I should do next. I am even worse as a flirtee. I have an urge to giggle stupidly, which I only quell by looking sullen and shifty, like a British youth in a dole queue.

Once in New York City I signed up for a Flirting Seminar. They have that sort of thing in New York City. They also have prostitutes who specialise in being women pretending to be men dressing up as women. New York takes the romantic requirements of its citizens very seriously.

The seminar was held on a Tuesday night in a classroom in a community centre. In the next-door classroom was a group therapy session for single women who allow their domestic pets to interfere with their romantic lives. It was called "Sometimes Mr Tabby has to come second." And it's true – sometimes Mr Tabby *does* have to come second.

The seminar leader was a lady of uncertain age named Jessica. Jessica took us through the steps of Basic Flirtation. Jessica's instructions were very precise.

Jessica's 5-step programme

Step 1: Look the flirtee in the eye.

Step 2: Smile and use the flirtee's name.

Step 3: Pay compliments, with a smile in your voice, and if possible touch the flirtee on the arm while sharing a joke.

Step 4: Ask the flirtee questions.

Step 5: Use the secret weapon.

The secret weapon was Jessica's patented deal-clincher. This is to be used when you are not just flirting, but looking to Get That Date. She looked us all in the eye – a trick I assume you learn in the advanced Group Flirting class – and lowered her voice. We leaned forward. Some of us held our breath. "Little pauses," said Jessica.

Jessica demonstrated. She stepped toward me and lightly touched my wrist. It was a touch like the spring breeze stirring the new leaves of the jacaranda. She smiled. She looked up from beneath her lashes. Her eyes were dancing, not like Michael Flatley or even Michael Jackson, but like the sun on the sea in the early morning when you are standing on a hotel balcony having woken without a hangover.

"Look, Darrel," she said, in a voice like a swatch of velvet being folded, "would you, uh, like to get a drink with me sometime?"

The class burst into applause. My palms were sweating. My knees were quivering. I had to bend double to hold them steady. She was a genius. She was the Stephen Hawking of flirting.

"Now you try," she said. I tried. I did. I tried the eye-contact, but my eyes bulged like Homer Simpson's. I tried the light touch on the wrist, but my hands were so moist they slipped off and I had to grab her by the absorbent cotton of her sleeve. The slight pause before speaking made me resemble a Serbian general in a war-crimes court, listening to the translation in his earphones before deciding how to plead. "Why are you rolling your eyes like that?" demanded Jessica. "I'm trying to make them dance," I said.

We all received certificates to prove we had successfully completed the Flirting Seminar, although Jessica pursed her lips as she signed mine. I don't think she signed her real name. As I left, she took my arm and murmured some last advice. "The most important thing," she said with pity in her voice, "is to learn to love yourself."

I stood on the sidewalk outside. There was a moon over Manhattan. I took myself lightly by the wrist. Then I let go of my wrist. When you are learning to love yourself, you don't want to rush things. "So, uh, Darrel," I said, "would you, uh, like to get a drink?"

And maybe it was the free wine with the seminar. Maybe it was the moon, orange like a Chinese lantern. Because do you know what? I said yes.

Dating

"It is useless trying to impress women. If they are listening to you at all, they are already as impressed as they will ever be."

— CLIVE JAMES

THERE ARE SOME DRAWBACKS TO BEING SINGLE. NO, REALLY, there are. Sunday evenings in winter, for instance.

Every Sunday evening in winter when you go to the KFC drive-thru for a three-course Bachelor dinner to eat on the sofa while watching the eight o'clock movie, there is always a young couple in the car in front of you, and there is always something about his ratty old jersey and her hair tied back in a careless ponytail that tells you they are on their way home from an afternoon of reading the newspapers and throwing pieces of bread at the ducks in the park. You just know they are going to go home and eat chicken on their sofa and watch the same movie as you, only they will be together. And then afterwards maybe have sex.

At such moments the heart stirs. Even the happiest of singletons yearns for that someone with whom he or she can be thoughtlessly happy and eat fried chicken and watch the Sunday night movie. And then afterwards maybe have sex.

I generally console myself with the thought that when they get to the drive-thru window she is going to say, "I don't want any chips," and he is going to say, "Are you sure?" and she is going to say, "Yes, I'm sure," and he is going to say, "Well, okay, then," and he is only going to order a medium chips, which will be just the right amount of chips for him, and when they get home and settle on the sofa she is going to start eating his chips.

That usually does console me, but at other times, when I am unusually sensitive to the pellucid stillness of Sunday evening, I think, "You know, I wouldn't mind if my someone ate some of my chips. I would just order a large chips. I would order more chips than I actually wanted." The extra chips would be a small price to pay. I would think of it as my Sunday Night Happiness tax.

So, Sunday nights can be a drawback to being single, but even worse than Sunday nights is dating.

When you are single, you are sometimes forced to date. Dating is the devil's own pastime. Dating is about as much fun as drowning, or one of those movies in which Robin Williams sets out to prove to us that he can act as well as be funny. Ooh, dating is not fun.

At first I thought it was just *my* dates that were so bad. I believed that something deep and unexamined in my heart drove me to seek dates with nuts. I once asked a young lady out to dinner. She agreed to the date. She approved of the restaurant. Once we arrived, she perused the menu with appreciation. But when the waitress arrived, she said: "Oh, I won't be ordering. I don't like eating in front of people I don't know well."

My first thought was the thought of any young man in that position: "Wa-hay! I can afford to order the fillet for myself!" But my second thought was the thought that lingered: "Gee, this is kind of awkward." And it *was* kind of awkward, eating with someone watching the fork from your plate to your mouth. No one wants to be dating Gandhi. Well, *I* don't.

Nor was that the worst of my first dates. I have been to a restaurant with a woman who tried to persuade me to sneak out without paying. "Why?" I asked.

"It's exciting," she said.

"No," I said.

A few minutes later she stood up and walked out of the restaurant. I looked through the window and saw her running down the street. I don't know if she meant for me to follow her. If I ever see her again, perhaps I'll ask her.

I have been on a first date with a person who drank so much she vomited in my car. It doesn't get worse than that, you say? Did I mention that she vomited in my car on the way *to* the restaurant?

And I am still struggling to come to terms with the fact that I am like catnip to the sort of woman who, at a certain stage of the evening, will turn the conversation to the great pyramids of Egypt. "The pharaohs must have had assistance from else-where," they always say. "I'm not saying aliens necessarily …"

But it is not the weirdos you meet on dates that trouble me. Dating weirdos at least offers the hope that things might get better. Like, say, if you stop dating weirdos. What hurts more is the realisation that it doesn't matter who the other person is – it is dating itself that is so awful.

The fundamental premise is flawed. People go on dates to get to know each other better. Is there a worse reason to go on a date? Relationships are for getting to know someone, not dates.

There is nothing more guaranteed to quash the erotic impulse than learning about someone's unhappy schooldays, or how they never feel they have made their fathers proud, or how they always wanted to work with dolphins but now they are in public relations. Worse: if they tell enough, there is that awkward pause when they expect you to reciprocate.

Bad dates – when neither of you have anything to say – are bad enough, but good dates are worse. During good dates you are expected to say too much. I can just about bear to nod and make interested sounds when the other person is speaking, but when it is my turn to speak I always wish I were elsewhere. A Zimbabwe prison, say, or under the wheels of a bus. When you go on enough dates, talking about yourself becomes like perfecting a stand-up comedy routine. You know which stories work, which lines to use for which audience. The only person you bore is yourself.

And here's the worst of it: if it is a bad date, you go home alone and mooch around wondering what will become of you, but if it's a good date, what have you to look forward to? *A second date.*

But of course sometimes we have to date. And when we do, it is well to take precautions.

Have a plan

If you are the party suggesting the date – you brave person, you – have a definite plan. Do not find yourself saying, "Okay, great. Um, what do you feel like doing?" This will make you sound like one of those endearingly clueless secondary characters on an American sitcom. To be sure, that is better than sounding like, say, Anthony Hopkins in *Silence of the Lambs*, or Woody Allen, but the only place those endearingly clueless secondary characters get lucky is on American sitcoms. Do you live in an American sitcom? Right, then. Have a plan and stick to it. Then once you have extracted the requisite yes, exit the conversation. For now, things are as good as they are going to get.

Respect the conventions

We are all adults here. We know the courage required to ask someone out, especially when sober. It is our responsibility not to be unnecessarily hurtful. That is to say: don't be too honest.

Honesty is one of the most cowardly ways to be cruel. If you do not want to go on a date, the only decent thing to do is lie. Some ruthless individuals take it upon themselves to be honest. They say something like (let me see if I can remember the precise words … what am I saying? Of course I can. They are scorched on my heart in great letters of fire): "Look, I'm sorry, but I just don't think of you that way."

No one is grateful for that kind of honesty. A polite lie enables all parties to withdraw with dignity and some tatters of self-esteem still clinging, like the ragged shirt on a castaway's sun-blistered back.

Acceptable:

"That would be nice, but I am really busy at the moment";

"I have just ended a long relationship and I don't think I'm ready to date yet."

Unacceptable:

"Um, I'd really like to, but I'm not convinced we're not cousins";

"My numerologist says I shouldn't date for the next few weeks";

"You don't have to pretend with me. Everyone knows you're gay."

Of course, there are reciprocal obligations. Never press the point. If you press the point, you deserve any unpleasant truths coming your way.

Good response:

"Oh, I understand. Well, good luck with that. Bye."

Bad response:

"Okay, so when will you be free?";

"I can change, I know I can";

"Say, do you have any single friends?"

Should a woman ask out a man?

Ladies, you are right to be cautious. We are all equal now, but being equal does not mean being the same. The best way to invite a man on a date – as our mothers and grandmothers and their grandmothers before them knew – is to have him invite you and think it was his idea.

Some dos and don'ts of dating

- Men: **don't** think it is impressive to be overly assertive with the waiter. It takes a small man to push around some poor schmuck living off tips. Plus, he will spit on your food.

- Ladies: **don't** be honest about the food. If the man suggested the restaurant and you tell him afterwards the risotto was too gooey, he will feel like a failure. Beware of making a man feel like a failure. When a man feels like a failure, he goes off and sleeps with someone else until he feels successful again. The only acceptable way to say, "The clam chowder was too salty" is to swiftly follow it with, "You will have to come over and try *my* mussel pot sometime."

- **Do** switch off your cellphone. *Before* your first call.

- If one of you is eating spaghetti, **do not** try to replicate that sexy food scene from *Lady and the Tramp*. Spaghetti is not that long in real life. Plus, your date may not have seen *Lady and the Tramp*. She will become confused. "Why are you eating my spaghetti?" she will say. This will put the rest of your evening in jeopardy.

- **Do** dress appropriately. If you are older than seventeen, that does not include T-shirts emblazoned with your favourite band. That does not include visible underwear at any age. Or tattoos.

- **Do not** succumb to the temptation to show your date "the real me". Try to remain attractive for as long as possible.

- **Do** bathe before the date and apply something that smells good, but fellows, employ restraint. A gentleman considers cologne to be intimate apparel. A gentleman never smells louder than his companion.

- Ladies, please. Just let him pay.

- Unless all you want is sex, **do not** have sex on the first date. If, on the other hand, all you want is sex, having sex on the first date is just about the best thing you can do.

Exiting a bad date

A date is not a sentence. Sometimes it is barely a clause. Some dates begin poorly and steadily improve, but I have never been on one of those dates. Dates that start badly usually get worse. Cut those dates short.

First dates should happen during the week. If things are not panning out, week nights enable you to say: "Oh, what a shame I must go. Big presentation at the office tomorrow." If your date says, "No, you don't. I'm your boss, remember?" you know you have just made the second of two very bad dating mistakes.

You may be forced into more drastic measures. I have an especially disreputable group of friends. These are some of the ruses they have used to cut dates short:

- My friend Rob once feigned instantaneous amnesia. "Excuse me," he said to his date, "but who are you and why are you sitting at my table?"

- My friend Dave favours the epileptic fit. He flails and falls to the floor and foams like a cappuccino. Then he lies still for a moment and looks up at his date. "Don't worry," he says, "Julius Caesar was also epileptic. Can you smell toast burning?"

- My friend Janice has a foolproof manoeuvre. She will return from the bathroom and tell her date: "Oh dear, I think I may have just taken too much heroin. If I suddenly fall asleep, please telephone this number immediately."

- If my friend Evan wants to end his date very quickly, he starts telling the truth about himself. This has never been known to fail.

I am pleased I have friends like these. If worse comes to worst and I end up old and single, at least I will not be alone.

Bachelor's tip box:
If you haven't kissed by the end of the second date, you will probably not kiss.
If you haven't had sex by the end of the fourth date, one of you is lying.

Relationships

"There is only one love, but there are a thousand copies, all different."

— LA ROCHEFOUCAULD

OH, WHO KNOWS ABOUT RELATIONSHIPS? NOT ME. NOT YOU, either, I would venture. Even people who have long-lasting and successful relationships know very little about them. "Luck", they say, and "Timing", and "Patience", and "The capacity not to think about the relationship too much". People who write books giving advice about relationships are the modern version of the snake-oil salesmen who travelled the rural settlements in horse-drawn carts flogging elixirs and unguents. People bought them because they needed to buy something.

My father once told me: "There is no point asking 'What do women want?' Find out what *your* woman wants, and try to give it to her." By that time he was in his third marriage, so he must have known what he was talking about. But one of the reasons modern relationships are so tricky is that we scarcely know what *we* want, let alone our partners.

Arranged marriages

It sometimes seems to me that the ancients had the right idea. Arranged marriages – that's the ticket. Relationships are just as much a part of the free-market economy as are other spheres of life, and operate under much the same laws of supply and demand and economy of scale. One of the curses of contemporary society is too much choice. This is as true of love as it is of breakfast cereal.

Our decisions are too reversible. Arranged marriages take away those variables that cause such agonies of indecision: "Are they right for me? Have I done the right thing? Should I hold out for something better?" With an arranged marriage, you just grit your teeth and make it work. Yep, I think it will be an arranged marriage for me. I don't trust myself to make the right decisions. Plus, the best thing about arranged marriages is that you never have to go on another date.

Bad advice

But although I have given up on expecting good advice about relationships, I recognise bad advice when I see it. Bad advice is everywhere. It is the air we breathe. Recently, idly doing what I like to call "Research" on my tax return, I took myself to my local bookstore. How bad could relationship advice get, I wondered. I did not wonder for long.

There was a book on the shelf titled *Sixty Steps to the Perfect Relationship.* I opened it randomly and gasped at what I read. "Step 17: Share his interests, and soon he will be sharing yours."

Have you heard more appalling advice? I am a realist, gentle reader: I know I cannot stem the tide of history. There is nothing I can do to reverse the Age of Advice. I would be content just to play some small part in undoing the damage caused by the muddle-headed commandments that clog our emotional arteries.

Today I invite you to overthrow the tyranny of Step 17. Today I say to thee: "Sharing is dangerous. Learn what to share, and leave the rest alone."

SHARING

Of course, there are different kinds of sharing. Some sharing is good. Sharing a dessert, for instance, can be delightful, provided you don't eat more than your share. Sharing a joke, or a walk in the late summer rain – these are examples of good sharing. There are examples less glamorous but equally good. Sharing the responsibility for changing the baby's nappies, or sharing your dreams for the future, or sharing the pain of misfortune – this is all good sharing.

But boy oh boy, is there bad sharing. Once upon a time I invited a new partner back to my home. That night we did a fair amount of good sharing. I woke the next morning to an empty bed and an unpleasantly familiar sound. I opened my eyes and found myself staring at the spot where the door of the en-suite bathroom should have been. The door would have been there, had it been closed. The door was not closed. "Good morning," said my new partner brightly, waving with her free hand.

"By all that's godly, shut the door," I managed to gasp before burying my head under the pillow.

"But I thought we were close enough now that we didn't have to keep anything hidden," my new ex-partner said later, as I handed her her coat and pointed toward the door.

I implore you: keep some things to yourself. Intimacy does not mean transparency. That is equally true outside the bathroom. By all means share that nightmare in which you were chased by a giant egg wearing a George W. Bush mask, but be sensible: don't share the erotic dream in which you eloped with the guy who comes around selling pies and sandwiches at the office, unless of course you actually *are* planning to elope with the guy who comes around selling pies and sandwiches at the office – in which case I have no further advice but to pack a thermos.

No relationship ever profited by full disclosure. Let mystery be your helpmate. Not, obviously, such tawdry mysteries as making him wonder where you were last Saturday night when you switched off your cellphone, but the kind of casual mystery that our grandparents understood was the real glue between the sexes. Much as we pretend otherwise, no one really wants to understand everything about our partners. If we did, we wouldn't need partners, except to hold the ladder in place while we change the light bulb. Talk, by all means, but don't talk too much. No one wants to spend their lives with Ally McBeal. I direct your attention to the poet Congreve, who not only gave good counsel but made it rhyme:

> *Women are like tricks by sleight of hand,*
> *Which, to admire, we should not understand.*

(Here, as in very few other pieces of sound advice, the word "women" can be exchanged with the word "men" without any harm to the soundness of the advice.)

Katharine Hepburn and Spencer Tracy never lived together. For more than three decades they lived in separate houses, four doors apart. When they moved, they moved to another pair of houses, four doors apart. I am not suggesting you try such a radical solution. You are, in all probability, not Katharine Hepburn, and I would be very surprised if your husband were Spencer Tracy. I am suggesting that you allow each other the luxury of separate interests.

Indiscriminately sharing each other's interests leads to disillusionment and resentment. Once, in my folly, I was persuaded to invite a girlfriend to Friday-night poker. She didn't want to play, she told me, she just wanted to share my interests and meet my poker-playing friends. After an hour of watching six scowling men drink beer, slap cards on the table and jeer at each other's misfortunes, she said plaintively: "Is this really what you do all night?"

"Yes," I said.

"You don't talk?" she demanded.

"We do talk," I replied. "I've just raised Chunko's bet."

She stared at me for a long time, with a new expression in her eyes. She was seeing something she hadn't seen before, and she wasn't sure she liked it.

Next weekend, she telephoned me. "Do you want to come shopping with me today?" she asked.

I couldn't tell a lie. "No," I said.

"But I came with you to your poker evening," she said. The walls seemed to close about me.

We went shopping. I knew that of all her interests it would be the least harrowing to share. Besides, how bad could it be? I have bought things before.

As I am now aware, there is the world of difference between buying things and shopping. "We'll shop for you!" said my partner brightly. At the first store, at the first pair of shoes, I announced: "I'll take them."

My partner laughed out loud. "When you shop," she said, "you do not buy the first pair of shoes you see."

By the third store the floor was spinning and I had the giddy sensation of falling. Passing shoppers looked suddenly evil, their features devilish and cruel. I began to sob silently. By the fifth store my sobs were no longer silent. "You're not making this enjoyable," snarled my partner.

I grew fearful, and cowered on the floor. Could this be the world my beloved chose to inhabit? This long, flickering, sub-terranean limbo, peopled by hobgoblins and trolls, sick with the scent of perfume testers – could she feel at home here? In a flash all became clear: I was in their lair, *and she was one of them!*

And then I ran. I dropped the packets and ran with the very Furies at my heels. I never saw her again, which is a shame as I really did like that first pair of shoes.

Do not make our mistake. There are many things that cry out to be shared with your loved one: an umbrella, a sofa, the last slice of lemon meringue. There are many that do not: a bank account, anecdotes about past lovers, the only comfortable pillow. We should all pray for the wisdom to know the difference.

I call on you to love your partners but to cherish the differ-ences between you, to open your hearts but to cling tight to necessary secrets. Let the bathroom be your metaphor: sharing your life does not mean sharing your razor.

Breaking Up

RELATIONSHIPS ARE LIKE THE MAFIA, OR A FIAT UNO: DIFFICULT to get into and even more awkward to leave. There is no good way to leave someone, and there is certainly no good way to be left.

The sad truth is that we very often behave poorly during a break-up. Break-ups, you might say, bring out the worst in us. This is certainly true when we are being left. When we are being left, we go through the recognisable stages of grief.

The 14 stages of grief:

1. Denial
2. Relief
3. Anger
4. Plans for revenge
5. Saying: "No, I'm okay with it, really guys. It's for the best. I can see that."
6. Heavy drinking
7. Late-night weeping and telephone calls
8. Pleading
9. Stalking
10. Acceptance
11. Trying to sleep with their best friend
12. More anger
13. Acceptance again
14. Promiscuity

Remember, when you have been left, it is good to seek emotional support from friends. But break-ups are like the first six weeks of pregnancy – do not tell people about it until you are reasonably sure it will last. Most break-ups unfold through a cycle of temporary reconciliations, and the patience of even the best of friends is limited. Too often we squander our emotional capital seeking solace through the temporary break-ups, and by the time the final split happens, our friends are sick to death of hearing about it. Ideally, the bank balance of emotional support should be placed in a 32-day notice account.

Doing the leaving

Most of us are very bad at breaking up with people. This is a good thing. Imagine what kind of a monster would be *good* at breaking up with people.

We are bad at breaking up with people because we are cowardly. We are also very afraid of looking like a bad person. So, when initiating break-ups, we end up saying and doing things we never intended, which not only cause the break-up to become protracted and convoluted, but generally ends up making us look like bad people.

Sad to say, the only sure-fire way to guarantee a trouble-free break-up is if you are not actually there when it happens. If you are, you are sure to ad-lib something that wasn't in the script.

Bachelor's tip box:
When breaking up, always stick to the script.

For your comfort and convenience I am offering a professional service. I call it the E-Z-Come, E-Z-Go Undating Agency. The idea is to remove the unpredictable variable – you – from the break-up scenario. We offer a variety of packages, tailored to your financial and emotional requirements.

PACKAGE 1:

For a nominal fee, one of our operatives will approach your soon-to-be ex-partner in the street or at a red traffic light, hand over a cardboard box containing returnable personal items, and say: "Look, it's not you, it's him, okay? Take care of yourself. Bye."

PACKAGE 2:

Our operative will take your almost-ex to a coffee shop in an upmarket mall, buy him a cappuccino and say, "Look, mate, she was recently involved in a long-term relationship that hurt her quite badly, and while you are a very special guy and she will always cherish the time you had, she just isn't ready for that kind of commitment. You know?"

Our operative will provide Kleenex, issue a reassuring pat on the back and wait around long enough to say: "There, there. Let it out. You'll feel better afterwards."

PACKAGE 3:

Our top operative takes your former beloved to dinner at a swanky restaurant. They dine on fine foods and champagne so French it comes with a beret and goes ooh-la-la when you open it. After a pleasant hour of conversation, our operative slides a brown manilla envelope across the table, stuffed with doctored photographs, faked autopsy records and a certificate to prove, conclusively, that you are dead.

Optional extras:

- documentation detailing the existence of your identical cousin, who shares your name and will be living in your home from now on.
- we have code-sharing agreements with reputable plastic surgeons and the national witness relocation programme.

PACKAGE 4
(ONLY RECOMMENDED AS A LAST RESORT):

We come round and kill you.

Sex

I LEARNT SOMETHING INTERESTING ON THE DISCOVERY CHANNEL recently. I learnt that hurricanes are more likely to occur on 16 May than on any other day of the year. Isn't that interesting? But more to the point: I also learnt that on average some 100 million acts of sexual congress happen around the world every day. Doesn't that just take your breath away? Imagine being the poor shlub who had to cold-call everyone in the world to compile those figures.

However you look at it, that is a lot of sex. The figure would probably be about half that if you excluded Robbie Williams and the Catholic priesthood from the poll, but it is still impressive. That means that every day there are at least 50 million people who are getting more action than I am. It makes me feel I am not pulling my weight.

Ah, sex. For some, sex is a four-letter word. For some, sex is a three-letter word. For some, sex is a French-letter word. Not for me. For me, sex is a word written in hieroglyphics on the underside of a block of sandstone that's too heavy to lift.

People like to go on about how sex in the modern times is very confusing, but the thing about sex that most confuses me is how other people seem to have so little trouble in finding someone with whom to have it. Everyone seems to be having sex. Vladimir Putin has sex. The contestants on *The Jerry Springer Show* have sex. That little guy who plays Mini-Me in the Austin Powers movies probably has sex. The Williams sisters have sex. (With other people, I mean. Or at least, I assume. I *hope*.) Even Britney Spears is having sex. I overheard another of those horrors on *Big Brother* complaining that it had been a long time since she'd had sex. "It's been six weeks!" she wailed. Six weeks! Six weeks is not a long time in my home. Six weeks still counts as afterglow for me. After six weeks I have scarcely finished smoking my cigarette and phoning all my friends to brag.

It was Oscar Wilde, I think, who defined sex as "the unspeakable in pursuit of the uneatable". Some people claim he said it about fox-hunting, but that just doesn't make sense.

One-night stands

Who am I to talk to you about sex with your partner? But for good or bad, there is still a lot of casual sex knocking about. (Of course, sex is seldom really casual – the great trick is making it appear so.)

One-night stands have had a raw deal in recent years. Consensual coupling for the sake of nothing more worthy than a good time is frowned upon, tutted over and, on at least one occasion in my own incautious youth, doused with water. Practised with care, however, the odd bout of the one-off mattress mambo can boost the spirits and leave your nose wet and your coat with a healthy shine. A good one-night stand is nature's Prozac, and that is the only kind of one-night stand worth having.

Bad one-night stands are one-night stands that leave at least one of the parties feeling unhappy, cheap, deceived. How do you know whether you have left the other person feeling unhappy, cheap and deceived? Oh, you know, all right. Deep down, you always know.

There are many kinds of one-night stands, and most of them are to be avoided. Sadly, the most common is the one in which both parties are cripplingly inebriated. **The drunken one-night stand**, besides generally yielding dismal sex, is most awkward the next morning. The courteous one-night stander never implies they have done something they regret. Never catch yourself the next morning saying any of the following:

- "Oh God, I'll never drink daiquiris again";
- "I hope I didn't do anything stupid while lying naked in bed with you last night?";
- "What's this sticky stuff on my sunglasses?"

Equally poor form is **The freeze-out one-night stand**. There is a distasteful subset of individuals who are all patter and smouldering looks in the wee hours, but next morning act as though nothing has happened. Worse are the sort who become aloof and formal, with the air of someone trying to be polite to a war veteran who has tracked mud into the bedroom while in the process of invading their farm.

The most important part of the decent one-night stand is controlling the messages you send. Perhaps the most reviled of one-off lovers is the **Call-You-Later one-night-stander**. Generally a man, although I notice with regret that women are beginning to muscle in on the scene, this is the cad who raises the false expectations of further contact.

Learn the art of the suave generality. Say: "You are beautiful," if you must, rather than "You are the most beautiful person I have ever met." Say: "I am pleased I met you," rather than "I am so lucky to have met you."

Do not deliberately mislead. If someone is having sex with you on your first night together, the reasonable assumption is that they understand it to be for one night only. If that is not the message you want to send, don't have sex on the first night.

Many Call-You-Later one-night-standers mistakenly assume that their partners necessarily repine for further dates and romantic walks on the beach. Feeling guilty, not wanting to be a cad, they bungle: they use the word "we", they imply breakfast on Sunday, they ask for a telephone number. If they lose their head entirely, they make a demonstration of saving the number on their mobile phone. Fearing looking like a cad, they become a cad. More wicked deeds are committed through weakness than wickedness.

There are some Dos and Don'ts you may want to think about.

- **Do not** wake up and start gabbling getaway excuses about your busy day or your mother's birthday. This is not courteous. You are both adults here. (If you are not, you have bigger troubles to think about.)

- **Do** put on underwear – preferably yours – or a bathrobe immediately upon rising from bed. This is for purposes of etiquette, as well as the fact that you almost certainly do not look as good in the morning as your partner remembers you from the night before.

- **Do not** stay for breakfast, if you don't want to send mixed signals. A cup of coffee is, however, acceptable, polite and often downright necessary.

- **Do** briefly kiss goodbye, and make eye-contact. A hug is optional, but not necessarily advisable. Cupping her cheek in your palm and trying to look like Rudolph Valentino is not acceptable. Nor is lightly stroking his trouser region.

- **Do not** say something foolish at the door. "I'll call you" is criminal. "I hope we meet again some time" is offensive. "I'll see you around" is unclassy. Try something simple and timeless: "Thank you for a lovely evening" leaves anyone with a smile on their face. In sex, as in life, don't say more than is necessary.

Remember, almost all living creatures, with the obvious exception of certain unicellular organisms, jellyfish and Prince Charles, are capable of sex. What sets us apart from the creatures of the sea and beasts of the field is that we are capable of smiling about it afterwards.

Bachelor's tip box:
Do not say to your partner, "Honey, do you mind if I think about someone else when we make love?" Not unless you want her to reply: "Not at all. It makes a nice change. Usually when we make love you only think about yourself."

On the whole, the fundamental rituals and dances and feints and lunges of sexual pursuit probably haven't changed much over the years. A kiss, after all, is still a kiss, and a sigh is but a sigh. All the same, technology brings its own challenges.

Sex and technology

The human race is sadly predictable. Well, one half of it is, anyway. Take a close look at any invention sprung from the mind of a man; you will find, somewhere, the potential that invention has for increasing the inventor's chances of having sex. Otherwise that invention would never have been completed. It would still be lying at the back of a cluttered garage along with all the half-finished model airplanes and ships-in-bottles.

The male mind is ever ingenious, but it has no use for products that will not move the ladies. Think of the motor car, the zipper, the credit card. Consider the electric guitar, personalised license plates, hot and cold running water. All have their social uses, but all conceal their true purpose. If it doesn't make us look more powerful or attractive, if it doesn't make seduction a little easier, we just aren't interested. "A cake of soap that floats when you drop it in the bath?" the male inventor says, frowning. "How will that help me get lucky? Let me rather invent blue suede shoes!"

The same is true for the cellular phone. Marketers would have you believe that the cellphone's chief value is to summon help in emergencies or receive business calls on the move. This is not so. Had these been the sole uses of the cellphone, we would all still be carrying loose change and complaining that the public pay phones are always out of order.

SMS

The principal advantage of the cellphone is that it offers SMS. Oh, go on, you know what SMS is. SMS is the most powerful flirting tool since the invention of the eyebrow.

The essence of flirting is to appear to say much while really saying very little, or, depending on the time of evening, to appear to say little while really saying a lot. Flirting is an art similar to being an astrologer, or an economic analyst, or Naas Botha: you must at all times remain ambiguous. You must give the other person the opportunity to believe what they want to believe. The SMS, by these standards, is flirting personified.

The SMS arrives like a telegram – cryptic, staccato, stripped of syntax. It has the advantage over spoken conversation that you can end your communication with a question. If the sender is sufficiently skilled at the satin arts, it leaves the recipient in a happy swirl of speculation. I received a message the other evening. It read: "Am at such a boring dinner. You?"

Now what is a boy supposed to make of that? Is it a tacit invitation? A rhetorical question to fill a dull moment? Is the person writing this message at the table, or have they tiptoed off somewhere private? And mostly: what is the correct response?

I would like to say that I devised the perfect reply, all suave concision with the playful dance of ambiguity like the twinkle in Errol Flynn's eye, but I cannot tell a lie. After wringing hands and gnashing teeth and fruitlessly trying to phone more wily male friends for advice, I was reduced to such a craven state that I found myself laboriously writing "I'm eating pizza" and pressing Send. I didn't deserve a response. I didn't get one. I am ashamed to even tell the tale.

Almost as bad was the message I received a month ago. My phone beeped in the small hours of the morning. "I'm praying for you," said the incoming message. That's odd, I thought. I am not experiencing any emotional crisis or life-threatening illness. Why would someone be praying for me? Unless … unless "praying" is a synonym for "yearning", or "longing", or, oh mercy, "aching".

I was atwitter with excitement, the more so because I couldn't recognise the sender's number. It took me two days to pluck up the courage to call it, which means it took me two days to discover that it had been a wrong number.

Still, it doesn't always pay to be too smart with SMS. I have an especially villainous friend who makes a habit of stepping aside from social gatherings to write a message that says: "Someone's just said something that made me think of you. Remind me to tell you." He then sends that message to four or five female acquaintances. It seemed to work.

I suppose I am confessing that I am a bad friend when I say how delighted I was to be present on the occasion that he accidentally sent that message to two young ladies standing next to each other. But wait, it gets better: they were standing across the room from him.

Technology, as my old university professor was fond of saying, although he was referring to electronic typewriters, is only ever as intelligent as the person using it.

SMS ETIQUETTE

There really isn't much by way of SMS etiquette. SMS is a medium of communication principally used by teenagers. What etiquette do you think teenagers are going to invent? In lieu of etiquette, I urge you to maintain your dignity. We are not teenagers. We are grown-ups. We know how to spell and how to use grammar. That is what sets us apart from the beasts of the field, and the teenagers. Spell properly, damn it. Don't forget your commas and capitals. And above all, do not stoop to that weird phonetic code popular among the young. The only possible excuse for sending a message that says "UR gr8. CU 2nite?" is if you placed your cellphone in your back pocket and sat down without remembering to activate the keypad lock.

SMS SEX

When engaging in SMS sex, double-check the number to which you send your contributions. Double-check each time you send. Double-check again. I am not joking. Double-check. That's all I want to say. Double-check. I am not going to illustrate my point with an anecdote. The memory is too painful. Just please believe me: double-check.

CYBERSEX

There are people who have sex over the Internet. Don't ask me to explain it. Sex over the Internet is for people who find sex with prostitutes too intimate. There are very few sexual avenues I am not prepared to stroll down of an afternoon, had

I just the opportunity and a pair of stout walking shoes, but sex over the Internet is one of them.

I don't mean to be judgemental, but I just don't like the thought of it. I guess I believe that if I really wanted to have sex with creepy old men pretending to be busty blonde women, there are clubs where I could go to meet them.

(Before I start receiving postcards handwritten in suspicious fluids, let me take this moment to say that I am not interested in having sex with creepy old men pretending to be busty blonde women.)

All the same, to justify my research budget I decided to see for myself what all the fuss is about. I logged onto one of those Internet chat-rooms that offer what is optimistically described as adult conversation. "Adult" is one of those words and phrases that most often mean their precise opposite, like "democratic", or "You must come round for dinner soon", or "busty blonde woman".

I don't know if you have been to one of those chat-rooms. I hope you haven't. The one I visited was called Randy's House of Fun, or something. Randy's mansion had many rooms, and in each room you could talk with different types of like-minded people, each identified only by names like "Nine Inch Python" and "Holly Cumlightly" and "Anus Mirabilis" and "Honk if you like my hooters". I am not making these names up. Well, except "Anus Mirabilis". That one I did make up. But there are people out there who can have cybersex with someone called "Honk if you like my hooters" and not burst out laughing all over their keyboard.

I don't know how many of the women in the chat-room are really women. Based on what I saw, and drawing on what I know of men and women, and rounding up to the nearest whole number, I would say zero.

In chat-rooms you post a description of yourself, then idle around until someone sidles up to you and starts chatting. You can chat in public, or step away to a private cubicle where no one can see you … is this sounding pathetic yet?

I posted a description of myself, but none of the lovely ladies lingering in Randy's Love Shack seemed all that interested in having their way with a moody freelance writer roughly two pizzas away from moving up to the heavyweight division, should he ever decide to become a professional boxer. When it comes to finding a partner, the Internet is just the same as real life – the truth never helped anyone.

So I checked out and re-entered as Little Oral Annie, a twenty-year-old busty blonde air hostess whose dream it is to land a leading role in a touring production of *Cats*. Final proof, if proof I needed, that out there in the wide world are busty, blonde air hostesses with ambitions in musical theatre who are getting a lot more action than I am.

The boys were all over me like, well, like boys over a busty blonde air hostess with ambitions in musical theatre. The guiding principle of Internet sex, I gather, is to write down everything that you would be doing if you were having sex in real life. I would have expected more entries like "Watching television out of the corner of my eye" or "Counting the 9-times table backwards" or "Hoping what happened last time doesn't happen again", but the good men and alleged women of Randy's Passion Palace were all very focused on the job in hand.

The Bachelor in Love

Which led me to further puzzlement. Not to be too graphic or anything, but it is difficult to accurately portray the moment of sexual gratification in writing. I should imagine a persuasive way of conveying the fact that you have, eh, summited with Tenzing, would be to lapse into sudden silence, then yawn and switch off your computer. It is somehow not convincing to write, "Oh … oh, my golly … I'm … I'm about to …"

Or, worse, to write out the muffled sounds of sexual appreciation: "Aaaaaaahhh" or "Nnnngggggg" or "Unnnnffffff" or, not to give away too many secrets, "Oh, thank you, thank you."

In the length of time it takes to write all that – presumably one-handed – you could have reapplied your make-up and telephoned for a taxi.

I should have stayed and gathered material, but I just couldn't. I felt all dirty and soiled and just plain *wrong*. That's the same keyboard I use to write letters to my grandmother. Men – and I'm pretty sure that Throbbin' Robin and Powertool and Hunglikeamule really were men – can be repulsive. One glance at the horrors that Throbbin' Robin had in store for Little Oral Annie and I ran screaming, clawing at my own flesh and crying "Unclean! Unclean!" in a strangled voice.

It is easy to become despondent about sex in the twenty-first century, but sex in the twenty-first century is the same as sex has always been. Sex itself is simple. It is people that are weird. It is not even that people are getting weirder. People have always been weird, they are just finding new and more public ways of expressing that weirdness. In the course of my work – and sometimes the course of my leisure – I have visited swingers' clubs and wife-swapping circles and strip clubs and S&M clubs and I have spoken to adults who belong to True Love Waits, the organisation helpfully uniting people who pledge to remain virgins until marriage. There is nothing new to say about any of it. Sex is the potter's wheel upon which people turn the wobbly clay of their own personalities. If sex is mysterious, it is because we try to use it to explain too many other things. With sex, what you put in is most often what you take out.

The Code
of the Bachelor

I HAVE A GOOD FRIEND NAMED JO. JO IS A BACHELOR. JO HAPPENS to be single, although she was also a Bachelor when she was married. The marriage didn't end because she was a Bachelor. The marriage ended for the usual reasons that marriages end.

Every so often Jo and I meet and we have a few drinks and we complain about life. We complain about bad dates and broken hearts and breaking other people's hearts. We complain about other people and ourselves and the new *Star Wars* trilogy. We complain about having to go to social functions, and not being invited to social functions, and about people who use the phrase "Don't go there" and about why no one except Leon the barman can make a decent martini any more. We complain about growing older and we complain about the fact that we never seem to grow up. We complain a good deal and we sigh and mainly we don't really listen to the other person's complaints. We enjoy these meetings a great deal. They make us happy. Complaining about life is our way of expressing hope for the future.

Once a mutual friend horned in on our conversation. "You should appreciate life more," he said. We looked at him blankly.

"I do appreciate life," Jo said. "I just don't always enjoy it." There was a pause while we tried to decide whether that was a witty thing to say. "Now go away," said Jo to our mutual friend, "so that we can complain about you."

But after he left, we didn't complain about him. We sat pondering.

"I do enjoy life, on the whole," said Jo after a while.

"So do I," I said, "although I would enjoy it more if the drinks were cheaper. And if I could think of a way to finish my book."

"How is your book coming along?" asked Jo.

"I don't want to talk about it," I said.

There was another silence.

"Maybe we need a philosophy," said Jo at last.

"A philosophy?" I said.

"A philosophy," said Jo. "Maybe we would be more content with life if we had a philosophy. You know, if we had some consistent theoretical underpinning to unify our actions and reactions, rather than just doing whatever we feel like doing."

I thought about that. "But that would mean sometimes doing things that we really don't feel like doing," I protested. "A philosophy is a very big commitment. I have just bought a new car. One day I might get married. I don't know how much space I have in my life for extra long-term commitments."

"Maybe not a philosophy, then," said Jo. "Maybe just a code. Codes are easier than philosophies."

"We already have a code," I pointed out. And we do. If ever one of us is trapped in a boring conversation, we just scratch an ear and drop an item of cutlery on the floor, and the other will come over and rescue us.

"You know what I mean," said Jo. "If we don't have a code, how do we know if we should be happy with our behaviour?"

"I'm pretty happy," I said.

"So am I," admitted Jo. "But maybe we shouldn't be."

I pointed out that I didn't think the idea of either codes or philosophies is to find reasons to be unhappy, but I saw what she was driving at. It is good to formalise one's position on the world.

"It should be a short code," I said.

"Agreed," said Jo. "What are the principles by which you live?"

"I don't know if I would go so far as to call them principles," I said, considering. "But I do try to get through life with some sort of dignity."

"Really?" said Jo. "Drinking too many martinis and singing sad Sinatra songs on Leon the barman's karaoke machine whenever you break up with someone? Do you consider that dignified behaviour?"

"Yes," I said. "If I had been singing Phil Collins songs, *that* would not have been dignified behaviour."

"I hope that is not an example of the material you are using in your book."

"Okay, if I had been at whatsername's place, begging her to take me back and promising to change whatever it was she wanted me to change, just because I was afraid of being on my own – *that* would have been undignified behaviour."

"*Are* you afraid of being on your own?"

"Sometimes."

We sat and sipped our drinks and tried to think of a workable code for Bachelor living.

"How about this," said Jo at last. "How about: 'First do no harm.'"

"'First do no harm'?" I said. "But that's from the Hippocratic oath. That's for doctors, not Bachelors."

"Yes," said Jo, "but that's really all we need. Because it includes us too. Doing no harm includes doing no harm to yourself, see? That's what you're trying to say with that 'dignity' guff."

"Hmm," I said. "But this doing no harm to ourselves – does it include smoking and drinking and staying out too late the night before a big meeting? Does it include not taking the videos back to the video shop on time because we are too lazy to get up and would rather pay the fine? Does it include dating inappropriate people just because we like them?"

"Oh," said Jo. "Okay, I see what you mean."

And then the waiter returned with our fresh drinks, and I complained that so few establishments chill their beer glasses any more and Jo complained about waiters who write "Have a great day!!!" on the bill, and we kind of forgot about the code of the Bachelor.

And outside the sky darkened and the great world kept turning round and somewhere, on the other side of the globe, the Naked Chef was rubbing his hands together and preparing to dice a leek. And then, just like that, another day was done.